D1563827

The proceeds from the sale of this book will be used to support the mission of Library of America, a nonprofit organization that champions the nation's cultural heritage by publishing America's greatest writing in authoritative new editions and providing resources for readers to explore this rich, living legacy.

ROBERT FROST
SIXTEEN POEMS TO LEARN
BY HEART

Also by Jay Parini

FICTION
The Damascus Road
The Passages of H.M.
The Apprentice Lover
Benjamin's Crossing
Bay of Arrows
The Last Station
The Patch Boys
The Love Run

POETRY
New and Collected Poems: 1975–2015
The Art of Subtraction: New and Selected Poems
House of Days
Town Life
Anthracite Country
Singing in Time

NONFICTION AND CRITICISM
The Way of Jesus: Living a Spiritual and Ethical Life
Empire of Self: A Live of Gore Vidal
Jesus: The Human Face of God
Promised Land: Thirteen Books That Changed America
Why Poetry Matters
The Art of Teaching
One Matchless Time: A Life of William Faulkner
Robert Frost: A Life
Some Necessary Angels: Essays on Writing and Politics
John Steinbeck: A Biography
An Invitation to Poetry
Theodore Roethke: An American Romantic
Borges and Me: An Encounter

ROBERT FROST
SIXTEEN POEMS
TO LEARN BY HEART

Jay Parini

LIBRARY OF AMERICA

Designed and typeset by Gopa & Ted2, Inc.

Distributed to the trade in the United States
by Penguin Random House Inc.
and in Canada by Penguin Random House Canada Ltd.

Library of Congress Control Number: 2023945514
ISBN 978–1–59853–770–3

1 3 5 7 9 10 8 6 4 2

Printed in the United States of America

Robert Frost: Sixteen Poems to Learn by Heart
is published with support from

ELIZABETH W. SMITH

in memory of her father

SIDNEY JAMES WEINBERG JR.

Contents

INTRODUCTION

DURING A PUBLIC READING, Robert Frost was once asked why he so frequently recited his poems from memory. With typical wit, he replied: "If they won't stick to me, I won't stick to them." Remarkably among the modern poets, his poems "stick" to the reader. They find a way into memory, and they stay there, irrevocable—some of his poems more than others, of course. This little collection comprises sixteen Frost poems that have made their way into the memories of readers over the past century, each accompanied by a brief commentary. They are poems to memorize, then to recite, over and over. And then to metabolize, taking them into the body and the spirit, absorbing their wisdom.

Like many readers, I first encountered Frost in the classroom. I was in the ninth grade in a small city in northeastern Pennsylvania when my teacher assigned "Stopping by Woods on a Snowy Evening" as the subject of a paper I must deliver in two or three days. She insisted that I memorize the poem and recite it to the class, then offer an analysis. The assignment surprised me, as I had never, before that moment, thought about poetry or Robert Frost, although I had seen him once—on television, at the inauguration of President Kennedy, when he addressed the entire nation: a white-haired old man who recited a poem, "The Gift Outright," from memory. I took a selection of his poems back to my house that night and leafed through them.

At the time, Frost was still alive—this was a couple of years before his death in 1963 at the age of eighty-nine—and I remember what it felt like to read him for the first time. "Stopping by Woods" stunned me, this simple poem about a man driving a horse-drawn sled through the winter woods of rural New England at night. The mode of transportation was new to me. You could pull a sled with a horse?! I didn't know much about snowy woods or rural ways. But I soon believed that a man could, indeed, stop his horse in mid-flight to wonder about the owner of these woods and "To watch his woods fill up with snow." I marveled at that idea, of the woods filling up with snow.

And yet the scene wasn't all sweetness, as the speaker is caught "Between the woods and frozen lake / The darkest evening of the year." That seemed frightening. The horse "gives his harness bells a shake" as he wonders "if there is some mistake." Why would a man just stop to listen and watch? Then came two lines that changed my life: "The only other sound's the sweep / Of easy wind and downy flake." Frost framed those lines in a way that carves them into your brain. The simple syllables glide into each other, becoming a system of linked sounds. Once committed to memory, the words themselves in this order stay in place, a perpetual source of refreshment and awe.

I loved the famous last stanza too. One believes, with the speaker, that the woods are "lovely, dark and deep." In other words, the loveliness involves both darkness and depth. And how could one not shiver with the idea that there were "miles to go" before the speaker could sleep? This journey through the dark woods seemed to stretch beyond the literal boundaries of this passage. The repetition at the end is magical: "And miles to go before I sleep, / And miles to go before I sleep." Now *this* was poetry, I thought, and I was smitten for life.

I got a similar feeling when I turned the page in the little collection I'd been given and came upon "Dust of Snow." (It's not one of the sixteen poems offered in this book, but it's certainly one that anyone can, and probably should, memorize.) It goes:

> The way a crow
> Shook down on me
> The dust of snow
> From a hemlock tree
>
> Has given my heart
> A change of mood
> And saved some part
> Of a day I had rued.

The simplicity of expression in "Dust of Snow" inspires awe, with its insistent two-beat lines and pattern of exact rhymes enhancing its memorability. Everyone has experienced something like this blast of snow from a hemlock tree that a stray crow has dislodged. The poem refers to those unexpected shifts of feeling that occur when something in the so-called real world interrupts the mind's interior solitude and forces a shift of mood. Frost is interested in how the world won't let us sink into our subjectivity for long. Something out there strikes, shaking us loose from inward moorings, insisting that we confront our existence. We all need this "change of mood" now and then. And this abrupt shift can save some part of a day we might otherwise have "rued" or disparaged. The world is saying: "I'm here! Wake up!"

It's difficult to choose sixteen poems from this poet's large and shimmering body of work. He struck gold again and again. He once said that his goal was "to lodge a few poems where they'll be hard to get rid of." But that was a kind of false modesty on his part. Frost was, in fact, an unusually ambitious writer, a poet who wanted to, and did, make a permanent mark. As he wrote to a friend early in his career: "I expect to do something to the present state of literature in America."

What Frost hoped to do was to capture the "sound of sense," as he called it, in poetry. That is, he wanted his poems to go to the heart of what makes for memorable language, finding the intimate contours of ordinary speech. He expected his readers to listen to his poems and recognize, in their cadences, the natural sounds of human conversation. Writing to his former student John Bartlett from England in 1914, he speculated on how this worked. The "sound of sense," he argued, was "the abstract vitality of our speech. It is pure sound—pure form." He said the ear was "the only true writer and the only true reader." That is, everything settles on the sound of words on the page, th.... unique flow, their cadences, and the way the poet has yoked these sounds to create a poetic effect. He was interested in getting at what he referred to as the "action of the voice," which he related to "sound-posturing, gesture."

The goal of this book is to encourage readers to listen to the words and phrases, to locate their deepest rhythms, and to hear the tune of each poem as it unfolds. This is what makes the poems memorable. As ever, memory and understanding go hand in hand. Repeat Frost's words, say them aloud, listen closely, and try to comprehend them as well: that is the work of "standing under" the poems and taking in their meanings, which may be complex but which, over many readings, add to their shine. This deep reading, so integral to memorization, lodges the poems where they can't be easily removed from the reader's heart.

"We speak of memorizing as getting something 'by heart,' which really means 'by head,'" the poet and critic John Hollander once wrote. "But getting a poem . . . truly 'by heart' implies getting it by mind and memory and understanding and delight." Memorizing a poem can teach us much about its structure and argument, and about the resonance of particular words. Best of all, memorization makes a poem part of our inner lives. Once committed to memory, a poem is available to us for recall at any time—and the occasions for remembering it will make themselves known to us. It isn't something we have to work at. A line or stanza from "The Road Not Taken" may suddenly pop into the mind when we are faced with a difficult decision. Or, when hearing on the television news of the latest fire or flood, we may be moved to quote "Fire and Ice." It's not hard to find a place in everyday conversation or debate to drop the line "Good fences make good neighbors."

The man who wrote these sixteen poems—many of which were chosen by Frost to open or close a major collection of his verse—was a bundle of contradictions, hardly the simple farmer-poet he presented himself to be with considerable energy and success in the decades following upon the critical success of *North of Boston* in 1915. Yet he was, at heart, a poet who loved the common people he met during his years as a New England farmer. He was a loner by nature but one who liked company, a poet of isolation who nevertheless sought a mass audience. His devotion to his family, to his wife, Elinor, and to their children was admirable and sustained. And yet he often withdrew from them, seeking the solitude of his study or walking by himself in the woods. Home was, for him, hugely important—a place of refuge and a concept that had significant meaning for him; yet he traveled more widely than most writers, giving countless readings across the nation and abroad. He called many places "home," not only in Vermont and New Hampshire but in Massachusetts, Michigan, and Florida as well.

Even his politics were contradictory: he called himself a democrat, with a lowercase *d*, but he hugely disliked Franklin Roosevelt and his New Deal. He was no pacifist, and yet he appeared uninterested in the fight against fascism in the 1940s. He liked President Eisenhower a great deal, and yet in 1960 he campaigned with enthusiasm for John F. Kennedy. A man who passionately disliked communism, he was sent to the Soviet Union by Kennedy as a kind of cultural ambassador, where he met Soviet premier Nikita Khrushchev and called him "a great man." On and on, the contradictions multiply, making Frost something of an enigma.

Born in San Francisco in 1874, he was named after Robert E. Lee, the Confederate general admired by his father, William Prescott Frost Jr., a graduate of Harvard from a moderately well-off family in Lowell, Massachusetts. His mother was a native Scot, Isabelle "Belle" Moodie. She was a teacher as well as a devout member of the Swedenborgian church, with a deep strain of mysticism. Spirit and matter were, for her, deeply intertwined. Frost's father, by contrast, was a religious skeptic. A newspaper journalist by profession, he died of consumption when Frost was eleven, thus prompting the move back to New England, where Belle and her two children (Robert and his sister, Jeanie) were taken in by Frost's paternal grandparents.

Frost excelled in school, sharing the valedictory honors with his high school sweetheart, Elinor, whom he married only a few years later, having dropped out of Dartmouth College after only a month and a half. After a couple of years at Harvard, he moved with his young family to Derry, New Hampshire, where (with financial help from his grandfather) he became a poultry farmer. While looking after hundreds of hens, Frost also spent a good deal of time in the woods, taking walks that he called his "botanizing." He often spent his mornings at the country store in Derry, where he listened to farmers trading stories around a woodstove. That's where, he later said, he first came to realize that one could find poetry in the speech of ordinary folks. And he would appropriate that speech, with its distinct cadences and mannerisms, in his poetry.

Frost was never much of a farmer. "I like to keep a farm in my back yard," he often said, emphasizing that it wasn't his primary work. Not surprisingly, he found it necessary to supplement his income with teaching. While still farming in New Hampshire, he joined the faculty of the Plymouth Normal School and the Pinkerton Academy, where he was able to delve into poetry more deeply and began writing his own. When his grandfather died, he was able to sell the poultry farm and, having a little extra money from his inheritance, take the children (daughters Lesley, Irma, and Marjorie and son Carol) to England. He and Elinor set up in a small house near London, then moved into the Gloucester countryside. During this time, he met several poets and writers, including Edward Thomas, William Butler Yeats, T. E. Hulme, Wilfrid Wilson Gibson, and Lascelles Abercrombie. Soon Frost began to push his own poems into the world—a lucky meeting in London with Ezra Pound, the American poet and literary entrepreneur, led to the publication of Frost's first two books: *A Boy's Will* in 1913 and *North of Boston* in 1914.

Published first in London, these two books quickly found a publisher in New York as well, and when Frost returned to the United States in 1915, he found himself already on the way to fame. Amy Lowell, a popular poet at the time, wrote an enthusiastic review of *North of Boston* in *The New Republic*, saying it was "the most American volume of poetry which has appeared for some time." She admired Frost's realistic portrait of New England farmers, and she understood that he had caught "the sound of sense" from their voices.

"I should like to be so subtle at this game as to seem to the casual observer altogether obvious," Frost said, creating a poetry that would appeal to the ear of even the most ordinary, untrained reader. One didn't have to be trained in the complexities of English verse to grasp what he was doing. He wrote in traditional and well-recognized forms: blank verse, rhymed stanzas, sonnets. The idea of "free verse" never appealed to him, being "too much like playing tennis with the net down," he often said. He focused on metaphors, which in his view lay at the core of all good poetry. And he wanted to go as deeply into metaphorical thinking as he could, as he noted in a talk published in 1931 as an essay called "Education by Poetry." There he said, "I have wanted . . . to go further and further in making metaphor the whole of thinking." He added, "Poetry begins in trivial metaphors, pretty metaphors, 'grace' metaphors, and goes on to the profoundest thinking that we have."

The daily work of farmers often features in his work, and he found there an infinite source of metaphors. He wrote about mowing a field of hay in "Mowing," about picking apples in "After Apple-Picking." He wrote about planting seeds in "Putting in the Seed." One of the crucial activities of any good farmer was, in spring, to mend the drystone walls separating one property from another, and that work became the subject of "Mending Wall." In each of these poems, strong metaphorical images arise, and Frost develops them in subtle ways. "Mowing" is about writing as much as mowing, for example, as when he refers to "the earnest love that laid the swale in rows," which is not unlike putting down lines of poetry. "Hyla Brook" is about what could be called writer's block and how creativity can drift out of sight for a while, much as a stream will grow invisible for a time, "gone groping underground." "After Apple-Picking" is also about writing, dwelling on the creative exhaustion that can result from overwork. "Putting in the Seed" is about many things, but it has an obvious sexual allusion. "Stopping by Woods on a Snowy Evening" is, in part, about the isolation of the artist, a man who appreciates that the woods themselves— the woods of the imagination—are "lovely" on the one hand but "dark and deep" on the other. "Mending Wall" is a poem about the boundaries that become essential to the produc-tion of art, though it's a poem about literally fixing a wall that has been battered by winter frost and hunters. Every poem by Frost is about many things, but these elements work together in parallel interpretive directions.

Among the modern poets, Frost was a pastoral writer in the tradition of Theocritus and Virgil, the Greek and Latin poets of farming and rural life who Frost himself read closely, hav-ing studied classical languages in high school and college. The idea of pastoral verse is worth thinking about carefully. It's not poetry written by rural folks for rural folks; it is poetry writ-ten by sophisticated writers for an educated audience, one that has some familiarity with the conventions of poetry. One can enjoy Frost's work on many levels, but a full and sophisticated appreciation requires an awareness of his classical training and the traditions of English poetry. A close reading of his work reveals echoes of earlier writers, such as Shakespeare, Keats, Wordsworth, Emerson, and Dickinson. While Frost never wore his learning on his shirtsleeves, as did T. S. Eliot or Ezra Pound, his contemporaries, he was every bit as learned as they were, and—there is an irony here—he became a favorite on campuses throughout his adult life.

Frost taught at many colleges and universities, although Amherst became a kind of second home while he lived on a series of farms in New Hampshire and Vermont. The academy loved Frost and his work, and he found favor in classrooms across the nation. Although he never graduated from any college, he eventually received over forty honorary degrees. And critics flocked to him: he won the Pulitzer Prize four times, for instance, and there was never any shortage of commentary on his work in the public press or learned journals. "Frost is the dean of living U.S. poets," wrote an anonymous critic in *Time* on the publication of his monumental *Collected Poems* in 1949, "by virtue of age and achievement." A writer in the *Atlantic Monthly* described his poems as "not so much simple as elemental," suggesting that Frost "is uncompromisingly aware of an agonizing universe and creates apocalyptic twentieth-century visions no less grim than Hardy, Yeats, Eliot, and Auden."

It's easy to miss the vast range of Frost's work, from simple pastoral poems like "Mowing" or "The Sound of Trees" to brief aphoristic poems like "Fire and Ice" or "Dust of Snow" to longer dramatic narratives and meditative poems, such as the late and magnificent "Directive," which falls into the genre of the greater Romantic lyric. Among writers of narrative blank verse (unrhymed iambic pentameter), Frost ranks among the most skilled, as in "Mending Wall," "Birches," or "The Wood-Pile." He's also an artful sonneteer, as readers will notice in "Mowing," "Putting in the Seed," "Hyla Brook," or "Design"—the latter sonnet possibly the most terrifying piece of work that Frost ever wrote. For poems shaped in rhyming tetrameter (four-beat) stanzas, one can hardly imagine better examples than "Stopping by Woods on a Snowy Evening" and "The Road Not Taken." Finally, one should notice that Frost was a poet of love. "Reluctance" concludes with one of the most poignant stanzas in English-language poetry about the compelling nature of romantic desire:

> Ah, when to the heart of man
>> Was it ever less than a treason
> To go with the drift of things,
>> To yield with a grace to reason,
> And bow and accept the end
>> Of a love or a season?

Frost was also a master of the longer dramatic poem—a type of poem that reaches beyond the scope of this selection, as brevity and memory go hand in hand—but readers should dip into such poems as "The Death of the Hired Man," "Home Burial," or the withering sequence of five poems called "The Hill Wife."

These are fierce rural portraits of men and women at their wits' end who live in rural isolation on farms like those Frost himself encountered in the late nineteenth century in northern New England. Some of this drama will be found in 'Out, Out—' a poem of moderate length about the death of a boy while cutting wood on his family farm. It's a devastating portrait of subsistence farming, a world in which the simple loss of a hand could threaten the existence of a family.

The philosophical and spiritual depths explored in these poems are astonishing, often plumbing the darker sides of human existence. Strangely enough, Frost is often—too often—misread as a sweet homespun philosopher, a kind of folk poet. He actively cultivated this image in readings to large crowds. The critic Lionel Trilling heard him read, in 1946, at Kenyon College in Ohio, and he wrote disparagingly in his journal: "At Kenyon: Frost's strange speech—apparently of a kind that he often gives—he makes himself the buffoon—goes into a trance of aged childishness—he is the child who is rebelling against all the serious people who are trying to organize him—take away his will and individuality."

Thirteen years later, in New York, Trilling spoke at a birthday dinner for Frost at the Waldorf-Astoria Hotel, where he said: "We have come to think of him as virtually a symbol of America." But, he continued, "the manifest America of Robert Frost's poems is not the America that has its place in my own mind." He noted that only recently had he come fully to appreciate the complexity in Frost's work. "He is not the Frost who reassures us by his affirmations of old virtues, simplicities, pieties, and ways of feeling: anything but." Instead, Trilling believed that these poems represented "the terrible actualities of life," and he concluded—much to the poet's astonishment as he sat at the head table near the speaker—by saying, "I regard Robert Frost as a terrifying poet." Frost wasn't happy about Trilling's assessment, as one might guess. He preferred to keep the myth going, that he was a kind of simple farmer-poet; he complained to Trilling, not without charm: "You made my birthday party a surprise party." He also said, in a memorable line, "No sweeter music can come to my ears than the clash of arms over my dead body when I am down."

Frost was, to a degree, hiding from his real readers, those who would ultimately understand him as a complex and deeply ironic poet who plumbed the darkness of human existence. There is no doubt, of course, that he liked the idea of a popular audience, and it was true enough that his poems sold in large numbers. The collections poured out, usually every few years, and they rarely failed to find appreciative readers in large numbers on both sides of the Atlantic.

Despite his success in the world of letters, Frost was afflicted by dark moods. Although never diagnosed as such, he showed all the signs of manic depression or bipolar disorder. He would sometimes walk in the woods by himself for long periods (sometimes throughout the night) or sit in his study writing poetry into the wee hours as well as throughout the day. One sees this bleak mood embodied in "Acquainted with the Night," a stunning poem in every way:

I have been one acquainted with the night.
I have walked out in rain—and back in rain.
I have outwalked the furthest city light.

I have looked down the saddest city lane.
I have passed by the watchman on his beat
And dropped my eyes, unwilling to explain.

I have stood still and stopped the sound of feet
When far away an interrupted cry
Came over houses from another street,

But not to call me back or say good-by;
And further still at an unearthly height,
One luminary clock against the sky

Proclaimed the time was neither wrong nor right.
I have been one acquainted with the night.

Sleep, for Frost, could seem far away, an impossible king-dom. At other times, he could hardly lift himself from bed. He would remain in his room with the shades drawn for weeks at a time, refusing to come out. This behavior led to marital problems, as it would, and Frost's home life wasn't a happy one, although he remained loyal to Elinor until her untimely death in 1938. He had by this time lost two children in their early childhood and suffered from the death of his daughter Marjorie in childbirth. His son Carol took his own life in 1940.

And these were only some of the dark moments in a life that was full of bleakness at times. But Frost believed that there is "no way out but through"—the phrase occurs in "A Servant to Servants." And he lived by this wisdom.

Which brings us to the wisdom of Frost, which anyone who knows his work well must appreciate. Frost famously said in an essay called "The Figure a Poem Makes" that a poem "begins in delight and ends in wisdom." He compared this wisdom to the progress of love itself: "No one can really hold that the ecstasy should be static and stand still in one place. It begins in delight, it inclines to the impulse, it assumes direction with the first line laid down, it runs a course of lucky events, and ends in a clarification of life." Can any poet ever have written a better account of the trajectory that a poem—or the Platonic ideal of a poem—should follow from inception to conclusion?

A poem, Frost said, "must ride on its own melting," comparing it to "a piece of ice on a hot stove." One can visualize this. Reading a Frost poem, one sees how it flows naturally, finds its point of balance, "melts" into its meaning. We experience this "ride" and "melting" in "The Sound of Trees," for instance, one of his most sonorous and moving productions:

> I wonder about the trees.
> Why do we wish to bear
> Forever the noise of these
> More than another noise
> So close to our dwelling place?
> We suffer them by the day

Till we lose all measure of pace,
And fixity in our joys,
And acquire a listening air.
They are that that talks of going
But never gets away;
And that talks no less for knowing,
As it grows wiser and older,
That now it means to stay.
My feet tug at the floor
And my head sways to my shoulder
Sometimes when I watch trees sway,
From the window or the door.
I shall set forth for somewhere,
I shall make the reckless choice
Some day when they are in voice
And tossing so as to scare
The white clouds over them on.
I shall have less to say,
But I shall be gone.

Needless to say, the poet identifies with the trees in this poem.
Their rhythmic sway is utterly physical here. But the poem
becomes part of the body, as trees with their "noise" become
something we must carry or "bear." That we must "suffer them"
is such an odd choice of phrase by Frost. We endure the sound
of trees because they summon us, and we lose our "fixity," drawn
out by their energy, which is the energy of the spirits—Frost
knew, of course, that the word "spirit" comes from *spiritus*, the

Latin word for "wind." We acquire, in these moments of rapture, "a listening air." And this is what memorizing poetry asks of us: an attitude of listening, a receptive stance. We must make a close connection to the poem as a physical and moving object: "My feet tug at the floor / And my head sways to my shoulder." This is the balance required in taking on a great poem. You move with it, and it moves through you. It's a kind of dance.

Frost is a poet who takes us out of ourselves, then back in, where we rest in wholeness. We go out with him into the woods, into the swamp of "The Wood-Pile." We climb birches with him and ride them to the ground (in "Birches") knowing that "Earth's the right place for love." We stare into the well of memory and see ourselves: "Me myself in the summer heaven godlike," as he writes in "For Once, Then, Something." Finally, after a long and sometimes arduous and dislocating journey through a poem, we come at last to the stream that quenches our thirst for knowledge. And we know, with Frost (as he says in "Directive"): "Here are your waters and your watering place. / Drink and be whole again beyond confusion."

It may not be possible, of course, to commit all these poems to memory, especially the longer ones. But passages will stay in the mind, and they will return at unexpected times, a source of illumination, even wisdom. I don't know how many times I've repeated lines from his poems, even said whole poems. One night recently, during a sleepless hour, I found myself inadvertently reciting "Fire and Ice" again and again. A good poem is a prayer, and—like prayer itself—it brings us into conversation with eternity. We move from delight to wisdom, and we find ourselves at home. The poem offers a "clarification of life," as Frost wrote, and that is, at the least, something to provoke gratitude. Read these poems, let them sink into the memory, and let them help shape your life.

ROBERT FROST

SIXTEEN POEMS TO LEARN

BY HEART

ONE

Storm Fear

When the wind works against us in the dark,
And pelts with snow
The lower chamber window on the east,
And whispers with a sort of stifled bark,
The beast,
'Come out! Come out!'—
It costs no inward struggle not to go,
Ah, no!
I count our strength,
Two and a child,
Those of us not asleep subdued to mark
How the cold creeps as the fire dies at length,—
How drifts are piled,
Dooryard and road ungraded,
Till even the comforting barn grows far away,
And my heart owns a doubt
Whether 'tis in us to arise with day
And save ourselves unaided.

THIS SIMPLE, forceful, and terrifying poem appears in Frost's first book, *A Boy's Will* (1913), and it offers a vivid portrait of a young father with his wife and their child in a small farmhouse in the wilds of New England during a fierce blizzard. No names give the poem a specific setting, but we assume it's somewhere like New Hampshire or Vermont, as that's where most of the other poems in this volume are set. This is Frost's signature landscape: somewhere north of Boston, in a rural place. The poem shows Frost from the very first as a poet with a unique voice and vision, as if he were born full-grown, in complete control of his poetic technique, which here reaches a high level of sophistication.

The opening line is vastly memorable, almost a kind of earworm! "When the wind works against us in the dark" lodges itself in the brain, and it won't go away. How does Frost do this? It's certainly his major gift, the ability to frame a line that easily finds a way into the head and heart. This first is, in fact, a line of pentameter, but it's hardly regular, opening with an anapest, not the usual iamb. (That is, it begins with two unstressed syllables followed by a stressed syllable, rather than, as in an iamb, where we find one unstressed syllable followed by a stressed syllable.) The reader lunges forward into the poem from "w" to "w" to "w" in the first four words, as alliteration is employed with devastating effect. The monosyllabic thrust is powerful too: we feel nature pushing in, threatening to blow the house down, to overwhelm the family.

The melodramatic personification of the wind—it feels

like the Big Bad Wolf from the Brothers Grimm—is startling. This mythical beast shouts "'Come out! Come out!'" And the rhyme-word for "out" doesn't arrive until near the end with "doubt"—a way to keep the tension rising. This poem beautifully fits the definition of poetry as a system of linked sounds, and the linking devices include alliteration and assonance as well as end-rhymes.

Frost never wrote in free verse; indeed, he abhorred it, and usually stuck to familiar rhythms and conventional stanza patterns. But this poem nevertheless feels like free verse in that the lines are irregular, with only eight of them adhering to pentameter or at least five strong "beats." Only a single line conforms to the usual parameters of iambic pentameter: "It costs no inward struggle not to go." The other lines are a kind of "sprung rhythm," a term coined by the Victorian English poet Gerard Manley Hopkins, where he refers to counting "beats" or strong stresses instead of conventional "feet"—in other words, Frost allows for a wide variation in the number of unstressed syllables in a line, moving beyond the rigidity that can sometimes plague formal poetry. Throughout the poem, he controls the rhythms in a way that increases our sense, as readers, of being off-balance, even wrong-footed, and this enhances the theme of the poem, with a young family caught in perilous circumstances. Even the fire is waning, burning out, as the cold creeps in.

There are rhymes here, of course, and these are hardly slant or oblique: no word at the end of a line lacks a sound-mate somewhere in the poem. But this isn't a conventional type of rhyming, and the irregularity of the pattern again fits the theme of the poem: the wildness of the windstorm threatens to blow the place apart, even to blow the poem apart. The poet and his family are at risk, huddled for safety, and the comfort of a rhyme is hard to anticipate. The irregular nature of the form works together with the theme: a brilliant coincidence of form and feeling.

What's fascinating is that, even this early in Frost's career as a poet, he has found his mature, flinty voice. He marries this voice with the themes of human isolation and danger—themes that one expects to find in Frost's poetry through the decades. One could never in a million years confuse this poem with a poem by any other poet. The way the words hang together, the syntax, contains Frost's unique voice-print, as in "Those of us not asleep subdued to mark / How the cold creeps as the fire dies at length." The subject itself—solitude in a wintry landscape that becomes a symbol of threat—is something Frost will return to in later poems such as "Stopping by Woods on a Snowy Evening," "An Old Man's Winter Night," and "Desert Places."

As the beast-like storm "pelts" the windows and "bark[s]," seeking to enter the house and overtake the family, the reader feels the mounting anxiety of the speaker as well as his determination not to let anything bad happen to his little family. But there is no firm conclusion, no sense that in the final analysis the speaker will manage to hold off the threatening storm. Far from it. His heart "owns a doubt" that he and his wife can manage to save themselves unaided. Frost, of course, doesn't speculate about who would or could save them: God? A neighbor? Chance? It's all on them, the young parents, perhaps on the poet himself. The title of the poem itself tells us, the reader, that we've entered a place of uncertainty as well as terror. It's interesting that, so early in his writing career, Frost embraces his typical theme of human isolation and fear, with nature not as consoling but threatening, and with the world a place of disquiet and apprehension, with potential hazards always looming.

TWO

Mowing

There was never a sound beside the wood but one,
And that was my long scythe whispering to the ground.
What was it it whispered? I knew not well myself;
Perhaps it was something about the heat of the sun,
Something, perhaps, about the lack of sound—
And that was why it whispered and did not speak.
It was no dream of the gift of idle hours,
Or easy gold at the hand of fay or elf:
Anything more than the truth would have seemed too weak
To the earnest love that laid the swale in rows,
Not without feeble-pointed spikes of flowers
(Pale orchises), and scared a bright green snake.
The fact is the sweetest dream that labor knows.
My long scythe whispered and left the hay to make.

AN EARLY POEM, from *A Boy's Will* (1913), "Mow-
ing" was one of Frost's own favorites from this
period in his writing. This irregular sonnet shows his

grasp of a conventional form. It also shows his determination to take on and master a form that poets going back to the Renaissance era (one thinks especially of Petrarch) in Italy have regarded as a test of their technique. Of course, it's worth remembering that, in English, William Shakespeare himself prized the form, writing 154 sonnets that were published in 1609. And Frost would have had in mind great sonnets in English from Thomas Wyatt and Philip Sidney through Wordsworth and Keats.

The Italian sonnet pattern lies somewhere beneath "Mowing," and normally this type of sonnet contains an octave (eight-line stanza) that presents an image or scene followed by a sestet (six-line stanza) that contemplates or questions that image or scene. One expects the rhyme to go: *abbaabba, cdcdcd*. But Frost plays around with the usual pattern, bringing in elements of an Elizabethan (or Shakespearean) sonnet (*abab, cdcd, efef, gg*) but creating a pattern of his own: *abcabdec, dfegfg*.

The rhymes are exact, and the poem has the distinct feel of a sonnet, but the fourteen lines rarely conform to the usual iambic pentameter. Rhythms in English poetry are, in fact, rarely exact or regular: the language just doesn't operate in a tamed or tamable way. It makes little sense, here or in most good poems, to count mere syllables. It's a mistake to imagine that ten syllables make a perfect line of iambic pentameter. In fact, Frost blatantly refuses to worry about the number of syllables in "Mowing," as in the most famous line in the sonnet, where we will find eleven syllables: "The fact is the sweetest dream that labor knows." Frost counts only the strong beats, allowing the speaking voice to find and exploit a flexible five-beat line, using the rhythms to simulate the swing and swish of the scythe itself.

The opening line sinks into the memory as it begins the sway of the speaker in the act of mowing a field of hay by hand: "There was never a sound beside the wood but one." A mix of alliteration on "s" sounds and "w" sounds ("one" has a hidden "w" sound) and assonance secures the memorability. These elements are often present in a good line of poetry, and Frost uses them naturally, finding what he calls "the sound of sense" as he proceeds. Line by line, the speaker of the poem grows closer and closer to the "long scythe," which has a meaning it "whisper[s]" and the reader overhears.

This is a poem about making hay. In this, of course, one can't but help hearing "make hay while the sun shines," an old English proverb. There is a sexual allusion here too: making hay is making love, and "mowing" in English slang (going back to Shakespeare) often refers to the sexual act. But the more visible metaphor is that mowing is like writing. This "earnest love" refers to the work of cutting the grass in a swale (or field), but it's analogous to working at a poem, swinging the pen, cutting down language to fit into neat rows or lines of verse (*versus* in Latin is a furrow). A mown field becomes a poem in grass. The meaning that is "whispered" by the scythe may be "something about the heat of the sun," and this phrase alludes to Shakespeare's "Fear no more the heat o' the sun," a song from *Cymbeline*. That song ends so movingly: "All lovers young, all lovers must / Consign to thee, and come to dust."

The poem suggests that one should work steadily at the task

at hand, a "mowing" that is both literal and figurative here. Fantasy won't necessarily help, that "easy gold at the hand of fay or elf" one might get from fairy tales. This is hard work: standing in the field, swinging the scythe, finding a rhythm that yields piles of wet green grass that one allows to bake for days in the sun and "make," which is the act of becoming hay. One doesn't give in to fantasy but proceeds earnestly, sweating in the sun, perhaps smelling the flowers (orchids or "pale orchises") or scaring a "bright green snake" out of hiding.

This work of mowing or making hay or writing or making love is important because it edges closer and closer to the truth, toward reality itself, which is "the sweetest dream that labor knows." There is something noble that lives inside the mundane, and it's the work of the lyric "I" in this poem, the speaker, to uncover in the rhythms of mowing an intense physicality. The poem itself becomes a subtle enactment of its subject.

THREE

Reluctance

Out through the fields and the woods
   And over the walls I have wended;
I have climbed the hills of view
   And looked at the world, and descended;
I have come by the highway home,
   And lo, it is ended.

The leaves are all dead on the ground,
   Save those that the oak is keeping
To ravel them one by one
   And let them go scraping and creeping
Out over the crusted snow,
   When others are sleeping.

And the dead leaves lie huddled and still,
   No longer blown hither and thither;
The last lone aster is gone;
   The flowers of the witch-hazel wither;

The heart is still aching to seek,
  But the feet question 'Whither?'

Ah, when to the heart of man
  Was it ever less than a treason
To go with the drift of things,
  To yield with a grace to reason,
And bow and accept the end
  Of a love or a season?

"RELUCTANCE" is the concluding poem in *A Boy's Will* (1913), one that—more than the others in this selection—has an almost antiquated feel, which is partly due to the use of archaic or "poetic" phrases like "hills of view" or certain words: "lo," "wended," "thither," "Whither?" This diction draws on the repertoire of Georgian poetry— that written during the reign of George V, king of the United Kingdom, who ascended to the throne in 1910 (after the death of Edward VII) and remained as king until 1936. The poems associated with this period were often sentimental, with melancholic overtones, frequently set in the countryside, and always adhered to old-fashioned stanza shapes, such as the six-line rhyming stanzas of "Reluctance." Their rhythms were familiar, conventional, and—for the most part—iambic.

But this poem is Frost's own, the mature voice bleeding through the superficial Georgian skin and the mannerisms of this era, which predates modernist poetry. The setting isn't a surprise: Frost would often write in the voice of a man wandering in the woods by himself, so in some ways this early poem is a prototype. In this poem the speaker has been out for a long walk toward the end of autumn. He has been out for a long view, enjoying himself. But the season, which in New England can be quite beautiful, has faded, and in the first stanza the walk comes to an abrupt halt: "And lo, it is ended." There is a touch of melodrama here, of course: the end of a nice country walk can't be so bad, whatever the season! The use of "lo" feels slightly extreme under the circumstances.

But it's more than a country walk that has ended. It's a season of the spirit as well as a physical season. Suddenly we enter a landscape where personified leaves lie "dead on the ground," a massacre of leaves. This depressing image becomes a symbol of dejection. Only the oak—the sturdiest of trees—retains its foliage late into the fall, as if reluctant to let its leaves fly. Already there are patches of snow, or at least an imagined future snowfall, for the leaves to touch as they scrape along the frozen, snow-crusted ground. The personification continues in the third stanza, with the dead leaves "huddled and still" like small sleeping creatures who intentionally gather for warmth and protection. This kind of personification is commonplace in Georgian poetry, and Frost doesn't hesitate to use it generously here.

When Frost lived in Derry, New Hampshire (1901–11), as a young poultry farmer, he liked to get away by himself, hiking deep into the woods—he called this "botanizing." What he meant was that he was looking at the natural world closely, like a botanist, reading closely in the book of nature. Leafing through his poetry at large, one sees that he knew the specific names of the flowers, shrubs, and trees. He studied the sequence of seasons carefully. He knew the names of birds and animals, and he paid attention to their habits and patterns of migration. In "Reluctance," he shows off this knowledge, and we encounter the "lone aster" and the withering flowers of the witch hazel in the third stanza. These specifics move well beyond the typ·ical generalities of Georgian poetry. And they are typical of the mature Frost, who had a keen eye for nature's processes.

The final stanza lifts this poem to a fresh level of excellence and, indeed, memorability. The natural lyricism of Frost, of course, comes into full play here: when this poet opens the stops of his organ, the music grows large. This is a stanza I committed to memory almost fifty years ago, and it's been a surprising aid to my spirits ever since, a genuine piece of wis-dom that I realized—quite rightly in this case—would prove a benefit in later years:

> Ah, when to the heart of man
>   Was it ever less than a treason
> To go with the drift of things,
>   To yield with a grace to reason,
> And bow and accept the end
>   Of a love or a season?

That "Ah" pivots the poem into a fresh register, a wider focus. And the phrasing stays in the mind: "the drift of things" isn't something we like to govern our lives. That seems to suggest a lack of self-direction, an inability to stand firm. Like the speaker in Frost's poem, we want to have control over our lives. Reason is usually a good thing; but often we just don't want to be reasonable, especially when we don't feel reasonable ("reason" rhymes with "treason"). In the tug between head and heart, the poet wants the heart to win! With the phrase "the end / Of a love," there is now something else to consider in the poem. It's about feelings that matter.

We tend to cling to a past relationship, even when logically we know it's over. It seems disloyal to our experience itself not to do this. As for giving up a season: we don't want to let a season go if it's one in which we've been happy, even though we can see from the calendar that we can do nothing about the progress of time. Frost centers on this ordinary human conflict, and it's something every reader will understand as the poem moves from sadness, a sense of endings, a change of material circumstances, to a kind of resolution. The reluctance in the title is a reluctance to let the rational world overwhelm us. There is a drive to seize the wheel of our lives, and one identifies with the speaker here in his determination not to let "the drift of things" sweep him along.

FOUR

Mending Wall

Something there is that doesn't love a wall,
That sends the frozen-ground-swell under it,
And spills the upper boulders in the sun;
And makes gaps even two can pass abreast.
The work of hunters is another thing:
I have come after them and made repair
Where they have left not one stone on a stone,
But they would have the rabbit out of hiding,
To please the yelping dogs. The gaps I mean,
No one has seen them made or heard them made,
But at spring mending-time we find them there.
I let my neighbor know beyond the hill;
And on a day we meet to walk the line
And set the wall between us once again.
We keep the wall between us as we go.
To each the boulders that have fallen to each.
And some are loaves and some so nearly balls
We have to use a spell to make them balance:
'Stay where you are until our backs are turned!'

We wear our fingers rough with handling them.
Oh, just another kind of outdoor game,
One on a side. It comes to little more:
There where it is we do not need the wall:
He is all pine and I am apple orchard.
My apple trees will never get across
And eat the cones under his pines, I tell him.
He only says, 'Good fences make good neighbors.'
Spring is the mischief in me, and I wonder
If I could put a notion in his head:
'*Why* do they make good neighbors? Isn't it
Where there are cows? But here there are no cows.
Before I built a wall I'd ask to know
What I was walling in or walling out,
And to whom I was like to give offense.
Something there is that doesn't love a wall,
That wants it down.' I could say 'Elves' to him,
But it's not elves exactly, and I'd rather
He said it for himself. I see him there
Bringing a stone grasped firmly by the top
In each hand, like an old-stone savage armed.
He moves in darkness as it seems to me,
Not of woods only and the shade of trees.
He will not go behind his father's saying,
And he likes having thought of it so well
He says again, 'Good fences make good neighbors.'

"MENDING WALL" is the opening poem in *North of Boston* (1914), and it remains among the best of Frost's many poems, a poem that is read far and wide, at various levels of sophistication, by audiences young and old. It's a poem subject to misinterpretation, and it has been co-opted for political reasons, as people imagine that it either supports or rejects the notion that "'Good fences make good neighbors.'"

But it's a poem by Robert Frost. This means it's a poem full of ironies and complications. It's a playful poem, one that was never meant to deliver a political message, even a moral. Frost hated messages in poems. He would have agreed with the American playwright Moss Hart, who said that if you wanted to send a message, you should call Western Union.

Nevertheless, it's tempting to try to figure out whether there is a message of any kind and where the poet may have stood in relation to that message. After all, it's a poem in which two figures, New England farmers, come together, each on one "side" of the issue of whether walls are a good or bad thing. The speaker, vigorously, appears not to agree with his neighbor, whom he disparages as an "old-stone savage" who "moves in darkness." That is, he is a primitive, a cave dweller. We somehow imagine him inhabiting a world of deep prejudice, wishing to keep his farm, which is full of pine trees, separate from the apple trees of the speaker. These are two different kinds of agriculture.

Frost, who was himself an apple tree farmer in Vermont

for many years, might have written: "I don't like walls." But he doesn't do that. Instead, he says: "Something there is that doesn't love a wall, / That sends the frozen-ground-swell under it, / And spills the upper boulders in the sun." What is this mysterious "something" that dislikes walls and knocks them down? It's frost, of course. Frost disrupts the drystone wall, knocks the stones off their points of balance, creating gaps ("The lurking frost in the earth beneath," as the poet puts it in another, later poem called "Two Tramps in Mud Time"). But is Frost punning on his name?

He probably is, or he at least wants the reader to think he's doing that, and therefore that he's the disruptive element, the one who wants to pull down the wall. "Spring is the mischief in me," he says, in his wonderfully disruptive syntax. Note that he's actively courting the reader, trying to get the reader to imagine that he's a natural disrupter.

But wait a minute . . . does this work? Isn't the speaker the one who, once a year, summons his neighbor to this spring ritual of walking along either side of the wall and fixing the places where ground frost or perhaps hunters have created gaps that need repair? Frost writes: "I let my neighbor know beyond the hill; / And on a day we meet to walk the line / And set the wall between us once again." This should make us wonder now: What if the speaker didn't contact his neighbor, thus reminding him of their spring ritual of fixing the wall? Perhaps the wall would fall into disrepair. Perhaps the neighbor really doesn't care about fixing the wall. Would the speaker want it to fall into disrepair?

The question becomes: Why does he do this? Frost is playful here, as elsewhere in his poems. This antic quality suffuses his work. And he was a man who liked games, playing baseball and tennis himself for many years. He often said he was against writing in free verse because it was too much like playing tennis without a net. A net is like a wall, of course: it's a boundary in service to play.

The poem is written in blank verse: that is, unrhymed iambic pentameter, which is one of the most common forms of English poetry. It's not a rigid form, however: the first line, for instance, doesn't go ta-TUM, ta-TUM, ta-TUM, ta-TUM, ta-TUM. The first "foot" of the poem, in fact, isn't iambic. It's trochaic, going like this: TUM-ta. In Frost, the five beats of any line are more theoretical or notional than real. One can find them, of course, like five fence posts; but the beat is distorted by the speaking voice. Like any good poet, Frost lays the speaking voice over the theoretical meter, giving it a more natural feel. Indeed, "Mending Wall" is a fine example of Frost using the vernacular of New England farmers to create what he called "the sound of sense," making poetry out of rural syntax and turns of phrase, as in "'Before I built a wall I'd ask to know / What I was walling in or walling out, / And to whom I was like to give offense.'" This isn't "proper" English: it's a kind of regional dialect, which Frost himself learned by listening to those around him.

It's important to note that the speaker provokes his neighbor, taunting him by saying that there's no point to this wall, that his apple trees aren't going to walk onto his property and eat the cones under his pine trees. The neighbor puts up with this. He doesn't argue with his talkative neighbor and doesn't have much to say in return, and when he does speak, twice, it's only to give voice to the adage "'Good fences make good neighbors'" (something his father used to say to him). Indeed, these are the last words in the poem, which gives the adage its prominence. It's a deeply memorable and quotable line.

It's mistaken, I would argue, to identify Frost with the "frost" that disrupts the wall, with the talkative, more educated speaker who teases his neighbor and who looks down on him because of his prejudicial worldview. Frost wants to have everything both ways. He wants to entertain two points of view, and the poem becomes an area for the competition at hand. The poet sits in the bleachers with his reader and watches the farmers walk the line and toss ideas and competing notions back and forth. It's a game, but it's a game of knowledge.

It's also worth paying attention to the odd but enchanting title "Mending Wall." This almost sounds like a particular kind of wall, one that might be an aid to "mending" or fixing something. This is certainly a poem about making amends, of repairing relationships as well as physical barriers. And barriers can be useful, in that they often provoke a conversation. In the poem, this is so, even though the "old-stone savage" is taciturn, even a caricature of a certain kind of farmer, one who refuses to engage in dialogue but just keeps pushing forward his "father's saying."

The back-and-forth between these two farmers in "Mending Wall" is, in fact, an ancient conversation, one that invites us to think broadly about the meaning of walls or boundaries, ultimately finding in their preservation a kind of healing art, as in the saying "I'm on the mend." There is also a sense of replay in the poem as well as play as these two neighbors perform a ritual that makes for civilization itself, the repair of the boundaries that seem essential to them and the social world they inhabit. It's the act of walking along the wall that creates community for them, and the balance of viewpoints (the stones piled precariously on stones) seems necessary to sustaining a life for them both.

FIVE

After Apple-Picking

My long two-pointed ladder's sticking through a tree
Toward heaven still,
And there's a barrel that I didn't fill
Beside it, and there may be two or three
Apples I didn't pick upon some bough.
But I am done with apple-picking now.
Essence of winter sleep is on the night,
The scent of apples: I am drowsing off.
I cannot rub the strangeness from my sight
I got from looking through a pane of glass
I skimmed this morning from the drinking trough
And held against the world of hoary grass.
It melted, and I let it fall and break.
But I was well
Upon my way to sleep before it fell,
And I could tell
What form my dreaming was about to take.
Magnified apples appear and disappear,
Stem end and blossom end,

And every fleck of russet showing clear.
My instep arch not only keeps the ache,
It keeps the pressure of a ladder-round.
I feel the ladder sway as the boughs bend.
And I keep hearing from the cellar bin
The rumbling sound
Of load on load of apples coming in.
For I have had too much
Of apple-picking: I am overtired
Of the great harvest I myself desired.
There were ten thousand thousand fruit to touch,
Cherish in hand, lift down, and not let fall.
For all
That struck the earth,
No matter if not bruised or spiked with stubble,
Went surely to the cider-apple heap
As of no worth.
One can see what will trouble
This sleep of mine, whatever sleep it is.
Were he not gone,
The woodchuck could say whether it's like his
Long sleep, as I describe its coming on,
Or just some human sleep.

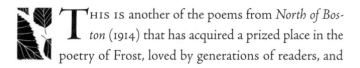 THIS IS another of the poems from *North of Bos-
ton* (1914) that has acquired a prized place in the
poetry of Frost, loved by generations of readers, and

with good reason. It's a remarkable piece of work, one in which Frost confronts many themes seen in the sweep of his writing from the most literal (in this case, the hard work of picking apples in New England during the harvest season of autumn) to the most figurative: it's on some level a poem about writing itself and, ultimately, a poem about hibernation and death.

It's Frost's version of John Keats's ode "To Autumn" (1820), a key Romantic poem in which the poet meditates in a series of affecting images on the fruitfulness of the fall, the hard work one associates with harvest—including the drowsiness that overtakes a harvester as the day moves on—and the season of death itself, viewed as winter on the near horizon. Keats looks toward the renewal of life in death, as the "red-breast whistles from a garden-croft" and "gathering swallows twitter in the skies." But Frost, ever dour in his way, stops short of that. "After Apple-Picking" is about sleep or death, perhaps resembling the woodchuck's "Long sleep . . . / Or just some human sleep."

The poem is another of Frost's few irregular poems. The line lengths vary, and one could think in looking with a casual glance that this was a free-verse poem, although the end-words have a rhyming mate somewhere, if not two of them. Roughly half of the lines approximate a standard line of pentameter; but the poet wanders between conventional lines and shorter ones, as if moving between wake and sleep. The speaker feels like the poet himself, and the poem represents yet another of Frost's celebrations of farmwork, this time focusing on the task of picking apples in the fall. Frost knows this subject firsthand, having spent a lot of time picking apples on his various farms in New Hampshire and Vermont, and he has an intimate relationship with this labor. He knows that special ladders are used, narrowing at the top, for instance.

And he begins with that "long two-pointed ladder" sticking through the treetops "Toward heaven still," but this is not a poem in the Transcendental vein. Frost's speaker doesn't wish to fly off into the sky. There is still an empty barrel below that needs filling. And so the task at hand can't easily be relinquished, especially as a few unpicked apples can be seen on the tree.

Whenever I read this poem, I think of Frost's voluminous notebooks, which are full of fragments of poems, odd lines, titles, aborted phrases that might, if lingered on properly, have been turned into poems. These are the unpicked apples in Frost's poem, apples he can't "Cherish in hand." They will ultimately fall to the ground, where they will be gathered into the "cider-apple heap," where they will be pressed for cider. One feels the frustration of the gleaner here, the apple picker who has worked hard all day but now must stop.

He is exhausted, is "done with apple-picking now," the speaker tells us as the poem begins to push into symbolic territory. This is, for me, clearly a poem about writing, about the exhaustion of the imagination, which can only push so far. "Essence of winter sleep is on the night," and this essence seems a kind of mythical summons to the dream-life of writing poetry. The speaker's nostrils fill with the "scent of apples," which sends him into a daze: "I am drowsing off." And suddenly he "cannot rub the strangeness" from his eyes that he "got from looking through a pane of glass" when, earlier in the day, he skimmed a lid of ice from a trough and held it "against the world of hoary grass." It's as if he's fallen now through the rabbit hole in *Alice in Wonderland*. Or imbibed a strong drug.

The world of apple-picking becomes almost hallucinogenic in detail as "Magnified apples appear and disappear, / Stem end and blossom end, / And every fleck of russet showing clear." These are dream-apples, growing in the imagination.

Memories of work and real life remain strong: "My instep arch not only keeps the ache, / It keeps the pressure of a ladder-round." Anyone who has climbed a ladder knows this ache, and Frost relishes the detail. The speaker continues to "feel the ladder sway as the boughs bend"—a willowy image, one in which the rhythm of the line imitates the sway of the ladder. The vivid imagery keeps the reality of the work before us, as literal and figurative continue to move in proximity. There is no sense of abandoning one for the other, although we have been told in the title that the poem is about "after" apple-picking. It's not about picking them in the present. It's certainly not about dreaming of the job to come. Everything is retrospective, but loud and clear: "And I keep hearing from the cellar bin / The rumbling sound / Of load on load of apples coming in." That is, the speaker can't or won't let go of the labor of the day. It was intense and meaningful. There was a good harvest.

The speaker has, it seems, done himself in by working hard, as an apple picker and a poet. This rings true in a biographical sense, as Frost was indeed wildly ambitious as a young poet, dreaming of literary glory, wanting to pick every poem/

apple from the tree of life. "Inflexible ambition serves us best," he wrote to a friend while in England as a young man. But the work has drained him, pushed him into a near-catatonic state: "I am overtired / Of the great harvest I myself desired." He reflects on the bounty that lay before him in possibility: "There were ten thousand thousand fruit to touch, / Cherish in hand, lift down, and not let fall." This is, in fact, the "world of ten thousand things" that Lao Tse talked about in the *Tao Te Ching*, referring to the great multiplicity of reality, the bounty of experience.

The poem moves toward an irresolute resolution. As the "Essence of winter sleep" overtakes the picker/poet, there is no clarity about what this sleep represents. Is it death? Perhaps. Is this the woodchuck's hibernation? If so, what does that mean for a human being? Is this perhaps just the usual sleep that follows hard work? What happens "after" the work of apple-picking is the subject of the poem, and Frost leans heavily toward the idea of winter. The grass, earlier in the day, was "hoary," that is, frost-covered. This is late in the fall to be picking apples. The poet seems to be losing his grip on reality as the "Magnified apples" lunge toward him and recede. The uncertainty here is intentional. Frost wants us to wonder what's going on, what sort of "sleep" follows from the hard work of life. He promises nothing, and that's the beauty of the poem—its willingness to face the dreaminess, the questions, the bewilderment that are part of human life.

SIX

The Wood-Pile

Out walking in the frozen swamp one gray day,
I paused and said, 'I will turn back from here.
No, I will go on farther—and we shall see.'
The hard snow held me, save where now and then
One foot went through. The view was all in lines
Straight up and down of tall slim trees
Too much alike to mark or name a place by
So as to say for certain I was here
Or somewhere else: I was just far from home.
A small bird flew before me. He was careful
To put a tree between us when he lighted,
And say no word to tell me who he was
Who was so foolish as to think what *he* thought.
He thought that I was after him for a feather—
The white one in his tail; like one who takes
Everything said as personal to himself.
One flight out sideways would have undeceived him.
And then there was a pile of wood for which
I forgot him and let his little fear

Carry him off the way I might have gone,
Without so much as wishing him good-night.
He went behind it to make his last stand.
It was a cord of maple, cut and split
And piled—and measured, four by four by eight.
And not another like it could I see.
No runner tracks in this year's snow looped near it.
And it was older sure than this year's cutting,
Or even last year's or the year's before.
The wood was gray and the bark warping off it
And the pile somewhat sunken. Clematis
Had wound strings round and round it like a bundle.
What held it though on one side was a tree
Still growing, and on one a stake and prop,
These latter about to fall. I thought that only
Someone who lived in turning to fresh tasks
Could so forget his handiwork on which
He spent himself, the labor of his ax,
And leave it there far from a useful fireplace
To warm the frozen swamp as best it could
With the slow smokeless burning of decay.

THIS POEM from *North of Boston* (1914), another early one by Frost, is written in classic blank verse, with some memorable lines encountered along the way as the speaker sets off for a solitary walk on a winter's day in a swamp. The setting could not be more Frostian! We enter the speaker's mind as he tries to decide whether to push on or not, and we experience the poet/speaker in the process of thinking as he goes. Anything can happen: "'I will turn back from here. / No, I will go on farther—and we shall see.'" This elaborate and explicit indecisiveness gives the poem its edge, as the reader continues onward with the walker. The poem itself becomes an adventure in the work of knowing, a journey into a space where learning is possible though not guaranteed. There is no solid physical or metaphysical ground here.

The controlling symbol is the swamp itself, where the hard snow on the ground—for all its glimmer of solidity—remains unstable: "The hard snow held me, save where now and then / One foot went through." This is, of course, the poem itself: "The view was all in lines / Straight up and down." These are the trees on view but also the straight lines of the blank verse the reader sees on the page; but the literal metaphor stays firm. The narrator summons a view of the "tall slim trees," which are, maddeningly, not distinct enough to lend a name to any part of the swampy landscape. The poet is "here / Or somewhere else." It's impossible to say. In a totalizing line, he says: "I was just far from home."

Home always marks a key symbol in Frost. It's a place of comfort but also danger. Frost moved around a lot, with his young family, from New Hampshire to England, then back to New Hampshire, then to a couple of different farms in Vermont. The Frosts bought a house in Amherst, Massachusetts—not far from Emily Dickinson's family home, in fact. There was hardly a stable "homestead" anywhere for Frost.

Home was, for him, "where . . . They have to take you in," as
he famously wrote in "The Death of the Hired Man." That's
hardly a home sweet home.

Now that the speaker in "The Wood-Pile" is far from the
potential comfort or threat of home, wherever that might be,
he allows himself to be guided by nature. "A small bird flew
before me," he says. The bird—an unspecific bird—says noth-
ing, landing on a limb, or perhaps a trunk, at a distance from
the hiker in the swamp. "He thought that I was after him for
a feather," the poet says, rather weirdly. This is an egotistical
bird, perhaps, one who thinks that the white feather in his tail
is just what everyone around him wants to seize and wear for
ornament. He is, says Frost in the vernacular syntax of a New
England farmer, "like one who takes / Everything said as per-
sonal to himself."

To a degree, Frost is making fun of himself here, I suspect.
"One flight out sideways would have undeceived him," the
narrator says, suggesting that a little distance from oneself is
remarkably educational. Perspective is everything. One gets the
feeling that Frost, the young unpublished poet on a farm in
New Hampshire, is talking to himself. He could get too deep
into his own head, and it was sometimes useful to take a step
"sideways" and get a different viewpoint.

Suddenly, and without much in the way of transition, we
come face-to-face with the major image in the poem, taking us
away from the distracting bird. "And then there was a pile of
wood for which / I forgot him and let his little fear / Carry him

off the way I might have gone." What do we encounter in the middle of a swamp? "It was a cord of maple, cut and split / And piled—and measured, four by four by eight." Frost shows us his country knowledge by giving us the measurements in exact terms. He'd cut and split and piled a cord of wood many times in his life, so he knows the labor that invariably goes into such a project. The image becomes a symbol quickly. A cord of wood is "measured" in the same way a poem is language that has been "measured" or put into measures. Remember that we're reading a blank-verse poem, which itself looks a bit like a cord of wood, lines neatly piled on lines of roughly the same length.

In the beginning decades of his life, when he had little in the way of public recognition—he wasn't remotely famous as a poet until nearly forty years of age—writing poetry was an isolated activity for Robert Frost. He wrote his poems for himself, far from public view. And now in "The Wood-Pile," the speaker stumbles on this mysterious cord of wood that sits in the middle of nowhere. "No runner tracks in this year's snow looped near it," which means it's been on its own in the swamp for a long time. It has been, in fact, several years since this wood was cut: "The wood was gray and the bark warping off it / And the pile somewhat sunken." Even the wild clematis has found a way to wrap itself around this bundle of sticks. Nature won't be held back for long. It's relentless, always trying to reclaim what was briefly lost. The "slow smokeless burning of decay" that Frost eloquently summons in the final line is part of the wood-pile's inevitable progress back to nature; the wood will, in due course, sink and dissolve into a soft mass, then soil, as it is broken down by insects and microorganisms. It's the nature of nature.

The ending, when regarded from the viewpoint of this being a poem about writing poetry, is poignant:

> I thought that only
> Someone who lived in turning to fresh tasks
> Could so forget his handiwork on which
> He spent himself, the labor of his ax,
> And leave it there far from a useful fireplace
> To warm the frozen swamp as best it could
> With the slow smokeless burning of decay.

One can imagine the poet at work, turning to the fresh task of a poem, working in seclusion. For the first decades of his adult life, mostly in New Hampshire on his chicken farm, Frost wrote without encouragement from editors or anything resembling a public. But he created poem after poem, always in fixed forms (such as a cord of wood), taking pride in the work he accomplished. Think of the oddness, however, inherent in the idea of a man cutting this much wood in the middle of nowhere and leaving it to rot. Why would he do that? What use could it possibly have?

We can't say, except that—when the writing analogy is applied—the madness seems part of the artistic process. A writer spends himself or herself in the lonely work at hand, is exhausted by the labor, and satisfied by the accomplishment for its own sake. The poem, in keeping with the analogy, is left "far from a useful fireplace." There is no voluntary reader in sight, nobody in need of what the poet might have to offer the world in the way of eloquence or insight. The poem is left on its own, in the middle of nowhere, to "warm the frozen swamp" in its glorious isolation.

"The Wood-Pile" is, finally, a poem about the wonder of art, and how artists create their works—poems, paintings, music, whatever—often in an isolated setting and without the hope of reward, without more than the dream of a "useful fireplace" where an audience might take it in. It's a poem about the single artist in the wilderness, a place where he or she will one day return to dust. It's a poem about the mad courage required in the act of creation. One builds a cord of wood, cutting the logs in an exact manner, piling them precisely. Then, the work of the poem begins or ends.

 SEVEN

The Road Not Taken

Two roads diverged in a yellow wood,
And sorry I could not travel both
And be one traveler, long I stood
And looked down one as far as I could
To where it bent in the undergrowth;

Then took the other, as just as fair,
And having perhaps the better claim,
Because it was grassy and wanted wear;
Though as for that the passing there
Had worn them really about the same,

And both that morning equally lay
In leaves no step had trodden black.
Oh, I kept the first for another day!
Yet knowing how way leads on to way,
I doubted if I should ever come back.

I shall be telling this with a sigh
Somewhere ages and ages hence:

Two roads diverged in a wood, and I—
I took the one less traveled by,
And that has made all the difference.

WRITTEN DURING Frost's stay in England,
then published in the *Atlantic Monthly* in 1915,
"The Road Not Taken" was included as the opening
poem in *Mountain Interval* a year later. It remains the best
known and least understood poem by Frost, endlessly quoted
and endlessly misunderstood.

Many of us have run into this poem somewhere, even if we
haven't "studied" it closely. I vividly recall one of my favorite
high school teachers in Pennsylvania, who had written out the
last three lines of the poem in her elegant hand and framed
them behind glass. The words sang out from the wall behind
her desk:

> Two roads diverged in a wood, and I—
> I took the one less traveled by,
> And that has made all the difference.

She often quoted these lines, saying to the class: "Listen to
Mr. Frost now. He's telling us to go our own way in life, and to
march to the beat of a different drummer. 'Do your own thing'
is the message." We all nodded in agreement, a warm feeling of
independence washing over us.

The problem, of course, is that it's not possible to believe in this reading—not if one has read the poem in a focused way, paying attention to key lines. Even if one has read it carefully, there are places in the poem where one scratches one's head: What is Frost really trying to say? It's worth noting right off the bat that this poem of four stanzas, each consisting of five lines and rhyming in a familiar pattern and proceeding with a four-beat line, seems to make a point about two diverging roads that contradicts the familiar conclusion, which is that the speaker took the less familiar road, the untrodden path, and this had a positive impact.

The poem begins with the famous line "Two roads diverged in a yellow wood." I doubt that Frost ever wrote a more memorable line. It's an indelible image, with autumnal yellow leaves in the woods, with the pathway branching at a fork. The reader knows the dilemma. (I always quote Yogi Berra here: "When you come to a fork in the road, take it.") That the path is symbolic feels almost too obvious. How often in life do we encounter this fork? Several times a day would seem a correct answer, and the choices before us can range from the most trivial to the most crucial. And we want, always, to have our cake and eat it; we hope to "travel both" and still remain "one traveler," although this is physically and spiritually impossible. We look yearningly down one path, then the other, attempting to read the tea leaves, to see into the future. The impossibility of this rarely gets in the way.

Frost's speaker looks down one road as far as he can, to the point where it disappears into the underbrush, then he "took the other, as just as fair." There's equality in the roads, isn't there? That's what the poem says. One is fair, and the other is "just as fair." The hesitant speaker questions himself, however, wondering if possibly one road might have the "better claim" to being less traveled "Because it was grassy and wanted wear." But the end of this stanza suggests otherwise, falling into an iambic rhythm that adds to its conclusiveness: "Though as for that the passing there / Had worn them really about the same." This may not seem definitive, but it's moving in that direction.

In case any doubt about the nature of the two roads remains, by the time he gets to the third stanza of this four-stanza poem, the poet seems without doubt: "And both that morning equally lay / In leaves no step had trodden black." This is wonderfully clear, wonderfully resolved. The way the alliteration works to link the two lines adds, of course, to their immense memorability. Frost puts the right words in the right order, and they stick in the brain.

I would suggest here that Frost's genius will be found in images like this, with the footsteps in the yellow leaves turning them from yellow to black by the pressure of the foot. Anyone who has walked in the yellow woods of autumn will know what Frost means and marvel at the succinct way he says it. This is a case of description becoming revelation. We see this. And it feels true. The language is suddenly without equivocation. These two roads are the same in their level of being worn. This puts the speaker into a newly anxious frame of mind. Whatever will he "do" with "the road not taken," the one he forgoes? This is, given the title, the ostensible focus of the poem. The speaker says: "I kept the first for another day!" But he no sooner makes this observation than he goes back on it, realizing how one rarely returns to a saved choice. Indeed, one almost can't. You can't go home again, as they say; home keeps shifting. It's never the same place. Rather, we ourselves are changed.

I often expand on the meaning of these lines when talking to students, telling them about a young man who came to my office one day with a dilemma. He was a first-year student at Middlebury College, my advisee, and he'd only been on campus a few weeks when he was having doubts about his choice. "I may be in the wrong place," he said. He had, he told me, been accepted at Amherst College but had declined their offer. He had called his mother to discuss his crisis, and she told him that if he still disliked Middlebury at the end of the year, he could always transfer to Amherst the following year. He wondered what I thought of that solution to his problem. I took Frost's poem off the shelf and read it to him, emphasizing the lines: "Yet knowing how way leads on to way, / I doubted if I should ever come back." I explained to him that he could probably transfer to Amherst for his second year. Why couldn't he? But it would never be the same as beginning there as a first-year student at Amherst. He would have made friends at Middlebury, and he would hate to leave them. He wouldn't have the same kind of experience as a second-year student at Amherst as the others in his class. You can't go back and retrace your steps. It just doesn't work that way in life.

The point of the Frost poem was well taken by my advisee. The poem's wisdom was clear. But the ending of the poem remained a puzzle to him, and it's a puzzle for most serious readers. As Frost pivots into that final stanza, he seems poised to give us a major dose of wisdom, as contained in the final aphoristic lines. "I took the one less traveled by," he swears. But how is this possible? He has already spent three out of four stanzas telling us that "both that morning equally lay" and that the roads were "really about the same."

The key to understanding this stanza lies in its opening lines: "I shall be telling this with a sigh / Somewhere ages and ages hence." Frost is suggesting that one day in the far distance, perhaps when he is a grandfather with his grandchildren gathered around his knee, he will swear that he "took the one less traveled by." He will maintain firmly that this act of independence "made all the difference." These words will by that time be part of a well-polished life narrative, the kind of story we all tell about ourselves. But, alas, he will know in his heart of hearts that he is faking it. He didn't know at the time which road was "less traveled." It's probable that both roads were the same. That strange "sigh" in the first line is one of regret, perhaps the loudest sigh in American literature. Frost, or his haunted speaker, knows that in saying he took the less traveled road, he will be lying. It's a pose. Perhaps it's a pose that he must adopt, and perhaps the lesson is still a good one. But Frost's speaker knows that he didn't at the time choose to march to the beat of a different drummer, as implied by the ending. He took a chance, launched in one direction while forgoing the other; that he came out well in the end was, if anything, a bit of luck.

"The Road Not Taken" was written toward the end of Frost's time in England, and it reflects on a walk in the coun-

tryside that Frost took with Edward Thomas (1878–1917), his
best friend during this period and perhaps the closest friend
that he ever had. (They planned to live side by side after the
war, perhaps in New England.) Though now remembered as
an important British poet of this era, Thomas was mostly a
journalist and reviewer when Frost met him; but Frost read
and liked his poetry, and he encouraged him to move in that
direction. They took long walks in the woods, hiking for many
miles, and once they happened upon a fork in the path not
unlike the one depicted in Frost's poem. Thomas was hesitant
and couldn't decide which was the right way for them to go.
Once a decision was made, Thomas kept regretting that they
had not chosen the other path. That was the origin of Frost's
poem: it was meant to tease his hesitant friend. But the situa-
tion had broader implications for Thomas, who was trying to
decide whether he should enlist in World War I, which began
in 1914. He had a family, was middle-aged, and didn't have to
enlist. But he did, in 1915, and was killed little more than a year
later, in the Battle of Arras, on April 9, 1917.

As ever, Frost was concerned in his poem with capturing the
speaking voice, and he does so with an almost uncanny sense of
the way speech unfolds, casually, moving one way, then another.
The rhythms aren't consistent, although most of them are
iambic at just the right time. A master craftsman, Frost knew
exactly what he was doing, and the reader should not assume
that anything in the poem is accidental. Even the ending, which
seems to deceive the casual reader, is intentional in its ambi-
guity. Frost doesn't want the reader to have an easy answer or

settle upon a moral that is without nuance. The poem has its own wisdom, which lies in the fact that the speaker knows that he will, one day, pretend to have taken the less traveled road. Indeed, there is a strong desire in each of us to characterize our choices in a way that reflects well on us. It's not for nothing that one of the most popular songs sung at funerals in America is Sinatra's "My Way." But we know, quietly and deeply, that every choice entails another, and every choice cancels another, and there will always be opportunities missed, whether through our decisions (good or bad) or circumstances that might have been otherwise. We're all haunted by other possible lives and roads not taken. They linger and trouble our sense of self.

EIGHT

Hyla Brook

By June our brook's run out of song and speed.
Sought for much after that, it will be found
Either to have gone groping underground
(And taken with it all the Hyla breed
That shouted in the mist a month ago,
Like ghost of sleigh-bells in a ghost of snow)—
Or flourished and come up in jewel-weed,
Weak foliage that is blown upon and bent
Even against the way its waters went.
Its bed is left a faded paper sheet
Of dead leaves stuck together by the heat
A brook to none but who remember long.
This as it will be seen is other far
Than with brooks taken otherwise in song.
We love the things we love for what they are.

UBLISHED IN Frost's *Mountain Interval* (1916), "Hyla Brook" is a lesser-known masterpiece, a brilliant fifteen-line poem that draws on the sonnet for its sound and flow. One could, in fact, be tempted at first reading to imagine that it's an Italian sonnet, as the first four lines fit that familiar rhyme scheme (*abba*). But the poem quickly slips into its own original form, adding an extra line, one of those zingers that burns a hole in the memory: "We love the things we love for what they are."

It's a poem about a brook, of course, and not a brook of any distinction. The small intermittent brook from which the poem draws its title wasn't far from the Frost farmhouse in Derry, New Hampshire, and Frost often walked along it, taking pleasure in its music. He felt decidedly possessive about this brook. It's "our brook." But by June it has slowed to a trickle, almost disappeared. By midsummer it's gone. But where? It's either "gone groping underground" as streams do, or perhaps gathered up into the flourishing but commonplace jewel-weed, transmogrified into "Weak foliage that is blown upon and bent / Even against the way its waters went."

I see this as another of Frost's poems about writing. A brook has long been associated with poetic inspiration, as with the Helicon, a stream that flowed in ancient Greece from Mount Parnassus, the home of the Muses. (Read Seamus Heaney's "Personal Helicon" in association with this poem for extra layers of resonance.) Writers all suffer from periods of drought, or perhaps—like many brooks in the summer—the inspiration just goes underground, out of sight for a while. A brook in New England often just sinks below sight in summer—a time when there is less snowmelt to feed its flow. The brook is still there, just invisible. The same goes with poetic inspiration. It doesn't disappear. It hides for a while.

The brook in Frost's poem disappears and takes with it the music of the Hyla breed, a kind of tree frog that lives near mountain streams and makes a marvelous sound in later spring. They "shouted in the mist" only a month before, says the poet. They're described as being like "ghost of sleigh-bells in a ghost of snow." That's a remarkable and memorable line if one ever existed, combining (even confusing) sight and sound in what is called synesthesia. The repetition of "ghost" is haunting. A ghost is white, whirling like a mist, part of the mist itself; the sleigh-bells are ghostly too. The snow itself is "a ghost of snow," not snow itself. All of this imagery is summoned to convey a sense of the song that the Hyla frogs once sang: a music that has been lost.

It's not hard to see the writing analogy:

> Its bed is left a faded paper sheet
> Of dead leaves stuck together by the heat—
> A brook to none but who remember long.

When the brook fades from view, what do we get? A paper sheet, like a piece of paper that might have once held a poem. This sheet is composed of "dead leaves"—one thinks of the "leaves" of a book here. It's a brook still, perhaps a poem still, but only to those "who remember long." Frost, of course, forgot very little. June for him was a melancholy month, the month when his infant daughter (Elinor Bettina) died in 1907—a harrowing experience for Frost and his wife, Elinor.

It could be said that Frost moved with the seasons, but that they often moved him into melancholy, even despair. Spring in his work is always associated with hopefulness, with renewal and transformation, as in his brilliant "Spring Pools," a poem where he sees in the oncoming summer a threat, as the trees in the spring "have it in their pent-up buds / To darken nature and be summer woods." For him, summer is a mixed bag: beautiful in its luxurious way but a prelude to autumn, to the dying world. As he writes in "The Oven Bird": "Mid-summer is to spring as one to ten."

One feels the dry throat of the brook in the "dead leaves stuck together by the heat"—an image of strangulation, suppression of speech. There is no impulse to song. "This as it will be seen is other far / Than with brooks taken otherwise in song." I read those lines as suggesting, in a glancing and decidedly obscure way, that Frost accepts as his own silence, ruefully; the brook has disappeared, but Frost is nevertheless aware that it will return one day. There are other brooks in the woods, some of them "taken otherwise in song." Yet he believes his brook will once again push its way to the surface. The poet's dry period, a period of depression and silence, a period of emptiness, will yield to something better, even "song."

Frost's nostalgia for the spring doesn't override his willingness to accept the moment for what it is. He remembers the old brook, and he can envision its rebirth. The last line in the poem—one of those epigrammatic lines for which Frost became famous—provides an aphorism that ranks among Frost's best: "We love the things we love for what they are." This is, on some level, a love poem, although the love is hidden here, out of sight. Frost's own marriage, to Elinor, was often tumultuous. But he loved her, and she loved him, and they remained together until her death in 1938. She did, however, blame him for the death of one of their children: Elliott died of cholera at the age of four, and Elinor believed that her husband hadn't done enough to help in the situation. (He'd insisted on waiting instead of calling a doctor at once.) And then there was Elinor Bettina, who died as an infant. One can sense the trouble over these untimely deaths as they emerge, fictionalized, in Frost's harrowing poem "Home Burial," where the wife can't understand her husband's seeming indifference to a child's death.

Frost was a realist, and he accepted the fact that mutability is part of life. This mutability finds expression in his ongoing portrait of nature's movement in his poems. We can't always have a song of spring, the brook in full throat, the frogs singing. Sometimes there is dryness. This might even be said of Frost's marriage, which ebbed and flowed. But Frost in "Hyla Brook" suggests that love remains despite the natural fluctuations, and that we love what we love because it's ours, it's there, and it's part of our world.

NINE

Birches

When I see birches bend to left and right
Across the lines of straighter darker trees,
I like to think some boy's been swinging them.
But swinging doesn't bend them down to stay
As ice-storms do. Often you must have seen them
Loaded with ice a sunny winter morning
After a rain. They click upon themselves
As the breeze rises, and turn many-colored
As the stir cracks and crazes their enamel.
Soon the sun's warmth makes them shed crystal shells
Shattering and avalanching on the snow-crust—
Such heaps of broken glass to sweep away
You'd think the inner dome of heaven had fallen.
They are dragged to the withered bracken by the load,
And they seem not to break; though once they are bowed
So low for long, they never right themselves:
You may see their trunks arching in the woods
Years afterwards, trailing their leaves on the ground
Like girls on hands and knees that throw their hair

Before them over their heads to dry in the sun.
But I was going to say when Truth broke in
With all her matter-of-fact about the ice-storm
I should prefer to have some boy bend them
As he went out and in to fetch the cows—
Some boy too far from town to learn baseball,
Whose only play was what he found himself,
Summer or winter, and could play alone.
One by one he subdued his father's trees
By riding them down over and over again
Until he took the stiffness out of them,
And not one but hung limp, not one was left
For him to conquer. He learned all there was
To learn about not launching out too soon
And so not carrying the tree away
Clear to the ground. He always kept his poise
To the top branches, climbing carefully
With the same pains you use to fill a cup
Up to the brim, and even above the brim.
Then he flung outward, feet first, with a swish,
Kicking his way down through the air to the ground.
So was I once myself a swinger of birches.
And so I dream of going back to be.
It's when I'm weary of considerations,
And life is too much like a pathless wood
Where your face burns and tickles with the cobwebs
Broken across it, and one eye is weeping
From a twig's having lashed across it open.

I'd like to get away from earth awhile
And then come back to it and begin over.
May no fate willfully misunderstand me
And half grant what I wish and snatch me away
Not to return. Earth's the right place for love:
I don't know where it's likely to go better.
I'd like to go by climbing a birch tree,
And climb black branches up a snow-white trunk
Toward heaven, till the tree could bear no more,
But dipped its top and set me down again.
That would be good both going and coming back.
One could do worse than be a swinger of birches.

IT'S NOT possible, with ease, to memorize a nearly sixty-line poem like "Birches," from *Mountain Interval* (1916); but so many lines and discrete passages stick in the mind that it's impossible not to remember them. The poem is a sinewy stretch of blank verse that, in fact, links several lyric sections—but without stanza breaks, making it a stichic, enhancing its free-flowing aura. The poem has its own swing, which mirrors of course the subject of the poem.

Everything comes back to the central image, which is that of a boy climbing birch trees in the wildness for sheer pleasure, riding them to the ground in a state of exhilaration as gravity takes hold. This isn't an unfamiliar pastime for children in rural New England, and the practice caught the poet's attention as a symbolic act that he could turn into poetry. The poem is among his most popular. Over many decades it was a rare public presentation when he didn't read "Birches." It's one of his "greatest hits," and it remains among the jewels of American poetry, a poem with a music of its own and distinct meanings.

The poem opens with three lines that I often say to myself:

> When I see birches bend to left and right
> Across the line of straighter darker trees,
> I like to think some boy's been swinging them.

I quoted these lines often during a recent ice storm in Vermont, when the white birch trees in the wood behind my farmhouse were tipped to the ground by heavy ice, bending left and right "Across the line of straighter darker trees"—the darker and straighter trees representing a hard reality that, no matter what you try, can't be "bent." The birch trees, for all their fragility, at least represent a medium that is flexible! And Frost, in this poem, sets out to explore that flexibility.

Having lived most of his life in rural New England, he knew that ice storms often bend down birches "to stay." This observation is a prelude to one of the most delicious passages in all of Frost, with its onomatopoetic diction—words that reveal in sound what they say:

> They click upon themselves
> As the breeze rises, and turn many-colored
> As the stir cracks and crazes their enamel.

The idea of trees clicking upon themselves stays with the reader. The intense visualization of these trees fits the definition of art as "an act of attention," as D. H. Lawrence once put it. Again, Frost's eye for nature was keen, and he writes with amazing ocular specificity about the trees as they "shed crystal shells / Shattering and avalanching on the snow-crust." The way Frost shatters the usual flow of the blank-verse line is breathtaking. Notice how he distributes the syllables here to create a feeling of instability, with a kind of lunging rhythm. Then he domesticates the wild image: "Such heaps of broken glass to sweep away / You'd think the inner dome of heaven had fallen." This is the ecosphere, the "house" of nature. (*Oikos*, the root word for "ecology," means "house" in Greek.)

With Frost, it's always worth remembering that he'd read much of the major poetry in English, and he refers to it in subtle ways. Poetry, for him (like most poets), was a conversation. Shelley wonders in his poem *Adonais* about the goal of poetry. Is it about pure and unlimited spiritual aspiration, such as that pursued by "the kings of thought"? Frost would seem to argue otherwise in "Birches."

His birches are "dragged to the withered bracken" by the weight of the trunks and branches sleeved in ice. The bracken are ferns, and there is something touching about their withered look. Summer is gone, and the triumph of winter is the triumph of death. The birches "never right themselves" and, for years afterward, a walker in the woods will see them drooping to the forest floor. This is the kind of local knowledge that this poet brings to the poem. But he is never satisfied for long with the usual imagery, and now he leaps into a strange sphere:

> You may see their trunks arching in the woods
> Years afterwards, trailing their leaves on the ground
> Like girls on hands and knees that throw their hair
> Before them over their heads to dry in the sun.

What? The image is arresting, of course. It's also erotic, signaling that the poem is, on some deep (and almost out-of-sight) level, a poem about sexual awakening. Indeed, the eros in this poem was never acknowledged by Frost. He probably never thought explicitly about this aspect of "Birches," but he certainly knew everything there is to know about metaphors and symbols, and he would deploy this knowledge without hesitation. From "Putting in the Seed" to a late and quite strange poem called "The Subverted Flower" (written in 1942), one sees buried or half-buried sexual allusions in Frost. But these allusions are never too explicit. It remains in the nature of a literary symbol to move in directions beyond itself, from denotation into further and further rings of connotation, and I won't press the erotic side of "Birches" too far. It's there for those who want to think about it. Even buried, it lends the poem an extra layer of meaning.

As ever, Frost's poetry moves like a mind itself, swinging from one topic to another, often abruptly (though guided by association). He notes in the poem that he wants to get back to the more "poetical" interpretation of the poem: "But I was going to say when Truth broke in / With all her matter-of-fact about the ice-storm." Truth, personified here, rudely interrupts Frost, here and elsewhere in his work. Truth is the reality principle, the literal image, which anchors the symbol. Frost keeps us alert, as readers, slapping us across the face now and then, saying: "Wake up! The world is what it is!"

A boy now arrives in the poem, an imagined boy from a local farm "Whose only play was what he found himself, / Summer or winter, and could play alone." He moves into the woodlot on his father's property and "One by one he subdued his father's trees / By riding them down over and over again / Until he took the stiffness out of them." There is something inevitably Freudian (or Oedipal) about this activity! We're given to understand that these birches belong to his father, and the boy wants to subdue them, to get the better of them, taking the "stiffness" out of them. The imagery, I think, speaks for itself.

The actual process of subduing his father's trees requires a certain knowledge, and there is skill involved:

> He learned all there was
> To learn about not launching out too soon
> And so not carrying the tree away
> Clear to the ground. He always kept his poise
> To the top branches, climbing carefully
> With the same pains you use to fill a cup
> Up to the brim, and even above the brim.

This young man (perhaps on the brink of manhood) must inhabit for himself the activity of growing, discovering in the process how to keep "his poise" as he climbs to the point where the balance shifts. He climbs as high as he can, until the tree can no longer bear the load, and then he lets fly: "Then he flung outward, feet first, with a swish, / Kicking his way down through the air to the ground." The rhythm of these lines embodies the act it describes, allowing us to see and feel the boy falling through the air as he flutters his way down to the earth. This is action writing at a high level, at once physical and metaphysical. And one can't help but repeat the lines again and again—they are just so perfect.

The tone now pivots as Frost brings himself, as speaker, into the poem: "So was I once myself a swinger of birches." It's a different poem from this point on as the speaker takes us back to his own boyhood. And he walks back through time, pushing through the harshness of his adult life with its tangled feelings, its tedium and confusion. When he is "weary of considerations, / And life is too much like a pathless wood"—an image that calls to mind Dante's "dark wood" and the Italian poet's own confusion in midlife—he delves into memory, recalling his time as a carefree "swinger of birches." It's at periods like this, in times of adult anxiety, that Frost's speaker declares: "I'd like to get away from earth awhile / And then come back to it and begin over." Hasn't everyone felt this at times? We can't travel for long through "a pathless wood" without feeling overwhelmed. We would like to lift off, like Frost, climbing to the treetops "Toward heaven still," as he writes in "After Apple-

Picking." We also like the idea of coming back to begin again, the dream of return.

In a whimsical, typically Frostian moment, the speaker says: "May no fate willfully misunderstand me / And half grant what I wish and snatch me away / Not to return." That is, he doesn't want simply to disappear into the ether. He's not a Transcendentalist, part of that mid-nineteenth-century school of writers who wanted to lift off into the beyond. The realist steps forward now: "Earth's the right place for love: / I don't know where it's likely to go better." These are, for me, the key lines in the poem, its moral center. This is a poem about the impulse to lift off into the heavens; but it's also about an awareness that love only happens on the earth itself. Love needs grounding.

At this point Frost moves into his great finale:

> I'd like to go by climbing a birch tree,
> And climb black branches up a snow-white trunk
> *Toward* heaven, till the tree could bear no more,
> But dipped its top and set me down again.

He puts "*Toward*" in italics, alerting the reader once again to the fact that earth is "the right place for love." One might wish to move in the direction of heaven but without continuing all the way into the clouds like Ralph Waldo Emerson in *Nature* (1836), where he fantasizes about having his "head bathed by the blithe air, and uplifted into infinite space." That's just too far, and Frost knows it.

As he often does, Frost finds an aphoristic summary line,

and this might be the most well-known of such totalizing lines in his work, a line full of a wry irony and charm: "One could do worse than be a swinger of birches." In other words, it's worth getting away from the difficulties of adulthood, the painfulness of mature love, with its attendant responsibilities and pitfalls. Climbing a birch tree is "good both going and coming back." Both directions speak to the necessary flow, the rise and fall, of the affections. "Birches" represents a quest for balance, a celebration of balance, and it enacts in its powerful swing exactly what it means, giving the reader a physical sense of the birch-swinger's trajectory.

TEN

Putting in the Seed

You come to fetch me from my work tonight
When supper's on the table, and we'll see
If I can leave off burying the white
Soft petals fallen from the apple tree
(Soft petals, yes, but not so barren quite,
Mingled with these, smooth bean and wrinkled pea;)
And go along with you ere you lose sight
Of what you came for and become like me,
Slave to a springtime passion for the earth.
How Love burns through the Putting in the Seed
On through the watching for that early birth
When, just as the soil tarnishes with weed,
The sturdy seedling with arched body comes
Shouldering its way and shedding the earth crumbs.

ANOTHER POEM from *Mountain Interval* (1916),
"Putting in the Seed" is a Shakespearean son-
net as well as a dramatic monologue, drawing strength

from both genres. It ends with a rhymed couplet that, in its totalizing image, gives the double meaning of the poem its resonance and memorability. That "sturdy seedling" that emerges from the soil with its "arched body"—a plant and, indeed, a child at birth that shoulders its way into existence, the result of an act of creation that comes from a combination of Love and Putting in the Seed.

Frost's speaker is a farmer, one assumes, as he speaks in a familiar New England dialect in that engaging first line: "You come to fetch me," thus creating a speaker and someone else, presumably the farmer's wife—although this relationship is implied, never stated directly. It's in the nature of a dramatic monologue to have a speaker, a listener/respondent, and some implied dramatic circumstances, and these are present here. "You" is being asked to come "fetch" or bring home the speaker "When supper's on the table"—presumably sometime later the same day. She has her work, he has his. It doesn't get more domestic. The energy of the labor at hand is such that one wonders whether, indeed, the farmer will allow himself the luxury of taking a break from this work of planting his garden, making it ready for plants that will burst from the soil in due course.

What is this task that so preoccupies the speaker? He's burying the "Soft petals fallen from the apple tree." Anyone who has seen these snowy and fragrant blossoms in northern New England in spring understands their glory. They sit in the black branches like snow. And they fall to the ground in lovely mounds that, in fact, gardeners love. The white petals make a great fertilizer, adding nutrients to the soil, and the farmer is burying them where he's planted "smooth bean and wrinkled pea."

The voice of the speaker is whimsical, as so often in Frost. He wants his wife to come back later, but he pretends to be afraid she'll be taken in with the work at hand and lose sight of what she came for and become, like her husband, "Slave to a springtime passion for the earth." (One can imagine their own "springtime passion" in bed, although that's distantly implied.) The way Frost's farmer talks about his wife suggests a kind of deep love for gardening, with its implied love for the work of "Putting in the Seed," which in its capitalized expression here becomes archetypal. And it yokes with another word in capitalized form: "Love." This combination tells us everything we need to know about this poem. It's a love poem, hence the choice of a Shakespearean sonnet: the ideal form for a poem about love, especially one with a lot of genial ambiguities, which is certainly the case here.

The poet winks at the woman, his wife, who winks at the speaker, entangling us in their unstated but implied desire for each other as well as their "passion for the earth." The poet understands that his farmer loves springtime too; this season of creativity has an amorous underside to it. It's a time for beginnings. He also believes that his passion for the work of farming is real: he seems to love this work of putting seeds in the earth so much that he might not even want to eat his supper. The literal and figurative meanings work in tandem here, as so often in Frost's poems. Form and content coalesce.

With a major volta or "turn" in the tenth line, the sonnet

heaves, more than simply moves, toward a marvelous conclu-
sion as "Love burns through the Putting in the Seed." This
is wonderfully physical, and I can't help but recall some lines
from Dylan Thomas: "The force that through the green fuse
drives the flower / Drives my green age." This is a primitive
force, one that involves the drive for procreation, and it entails
a wish to plant that is so elemental one almost can't describe it;
one simply gestures in its direction, as Frost does, believing his
readers will fully understand what he's trying to say.

The poem in the last four lines embraces imagery of birth,
and this is symbolism that can relate to both a child being born
and a plant pushing up through the topsoil:

> On through the watching for that early birth
> When, just as the soil tarnishes with weed,
> The sturdy seedling with arched body comes
> Shouldering its way and shedding the earth crumbs.

As usual, Frost has looked so closely at natural processes that
the particulars astonish in their visual detail. Notice how the
soil "tarnishes" with weeds. What a verb! And it implies years
of observation. The "sturdy seedling," whether a child or a plant,
comes arching its "body" as it shoulders its way into life. Frost
is making sure, of course, that the "body" has two meanings.
The baby/plant sheds "the earth crumbs" of its mother, forcing
its bold appearance in the world. The language itself, muscular
and memorable, catches fire in the final line, where the rhythms

seem to enact what they describe, the meaning pushing itself into the clearing, separating itself from the unconscious, coming into expression, fully embodied.

ELEVEN

'Out, Out—'

The buzz saw snarled and rattled in the yard
And made dust and dropped stove-length sticks of wood,
Sweet-scented stuff when the breeze drew across it.
And from there those that lifted eyes could count
Five mountain ranges one behind the other
Under the sunset far into Vermont.
And the saw snarled and rattled, snarled and rattled,
As it ran light, or had to bear a load.
And nothing happened: day was all but done.
Call it a day, I wish they might have said
To please the boy by giving him the half hour
That a boy counts so much when saved from work.
His sister stood beside him in her apron
To tell them 'Supper.' At the word, the saw,
As if to prove saws knew what supper meant,
Leaped out at the boy's hand, or seemed to leap—
He must have given the hand. However it was,
Neither refused the meeting. But the hand!

The boy's first outcry was a rueful laugh,
As he swung toward them holding up the hand
Half in appeal, but half as if to keep
The life from spilling. Then the boy saw all—
Since he was old enough to know, big boy
Doing a man's work, though a child at heart—
He saw all spoiled. 'Don't let him cut my hand off—
The doctor, when he comes. Don't let him, sister!'
So. But the hand was gone already.
The doctor put him in the dark of ether.
He lay and puffed his lips out with his breath.
And then—the watcher at his pulse took fright.
No one believed. They listened at his heart.
Little—less—nothing!—and that ended it.
No more to build on there. And they, since they
Were not the one dead, turned to their affairs.

"'OUT, OUT—'" may be too long to memorize in its entirety, but parts of this moving, powerful poem can be committed to memory with ease. It's written in blank verse, with a strong five-beat throb, and the details of the poem are vivid, the result of Frost's time on his farm in Franconia, New Hampshire, where he happened upon the story. Published in *Mountain Interval* in 1916, "'Out, Out—'" tells us about a boy (his age is never specified) who loses his hand in an accident with a circular saw while cutting logs for winter. The realism of the tale can't be doubted, as Frost perfectly describes every aspect of this accident, with devastating effect. I doubt any reader can get to the end of this narrative and not feel horrified, in shock.

One can hear this weirdly animated buzz saw in the yard as it "snarled and rattled," the words themselves sounding like what they depict. Frost opens with a bold gesture, giving life to this machine, which probably has been a recent acquisition on a preindustrial, subsistence farm. "The buzz saw snarled and rattled in the yard," we're told. And that line, once heard, can't be forgotten. Notice that the lines that follow create an atmosphere of beauty that, later in the poem, will seem like a distant idyllic memory. The "dust" from the saw is "Sweet-scented stuff"—the scent carried by a lovely breeze.

I've always loved the imagery that follows:

> And from there those that lifted eyes could count
> Five mountain ranges one behind the other
> Under the sunset far into Vermont.

This is perfect blank verse that plays with the underlying iambic rhythm but varies it to match the vernacular, the speaking voice. The speaker is looking westward into Vermont from the border of New Hampshire, where Frost's Franconia farmhouse remains, a place of pilgrimage for lovers of his work. One can easily imagine these five mountain ranges, "one behind the other," at sunset.

A long day of work draws to a close in the poem. Supper is almost ready. But that terrifying saw, possessing a life of its

own, keeps snarling and rattling. In the ninth line we are told—
reassured? — "nothing happened: day was all but done." The
adults in the poem might have called it a day, just "To please the
boy by giving him the half hour / That a boy counts so much
when saved from work." Then comes the boy's sister onto the
stage, letting them know their supper is ready. That would fin-
ish the day for sure. They're all hungry, ready to relax and eat.

But then, the saw reappears, personified, turned into a kind
of feral creature as it leaps "out at the boy's hand, or seemed
to leap." Frost wants us to dwell on the mystery—or perhaps
the muddle (a mystery has a solution, a muddle does not).
In times of extreme stress, during accidents like this, nobody
sees anything clearly or understands the elements or forces at
work. Confusion reigns. Who is responsible? How did this
happen? "He must have given the hand," says the narrator, as if
the boy would do such a thing. "However it was," the narrator
says, abandoning all hope of a coherent explanation, "Neither
refused the meeting." Does the boy have a death wish? That
seems unlikely. But Frost wants every bit of ambiguity he can
find. The accident happens in a blur, without clear motives; in
fact, it's a completely irrational and nonsensical situation. How
could a boy lose his hand in this way? Is the world so cruel, so
unyielding to human feelings?

"The boy's first outcry was a rueful laugh, / As he swung
toward them holding up the hand." What a terrifying image.
The boy's "rueful laugh" is believable, if unexpected. He proba-
bly went into immediate shock and felt nothing. But he knows

what happened and intuits the consequences. "Then the boy saw all," we're told (in an eerie way teasing the connection between the tool and the verb "to see"). The boy sees the life spilling from his hand, the blood gushing, his future falling away from him so quickly he can't begin to retrieve it or even think about retrieval. It's gone already, with the hand.

The doctor comes, but what does he do? The boy doesn't want him to cut off his hand to save him. A boy without a hand, he knows implicitly, would be a liability, yet another draw on the resources of a family at its wits' end as it tries to eke out a living. The hand is literal, of course; but it's figurative as well, as in a "hired hand." It represents a contribution to the family enterprise. "'Don't let him, sister!'" the boy cries helplessly, as the doctor puts a mask over the boy's face and puts him "in the dark of ether." This is, from a medical standpoint, a foolish move. The boy's in shock. His blood pressure will be low, falling precipitously. Ether was, of course, an anesthetic—commonly used in the early part of the twentieth century for simple operations. But it was, in this case, a medical gesture that perhaps kills the boy who "lay and puffed his lips out with his breath." Those gathered around, parents and siblings, the watchers at his pulse, take fright, as well they might. "No one believed," says Frost. "They listened at his heart. / Little—less—nothing!"

The boy is dead, and that's it. Indeed, the last lines have etched themselves into the collective memory of Frost's readers over decades: "No more to build on there. And they, since they / Were not the one dead, turned to their affairs." My students over the years have cringed at these concluding lines, seeing cruelty, not realism, in Frost and the farm family he writes about. How could the family be so callous? Didn't they care about the death of a child? Weren't they horribly sad and bewildered?

In fact, this family is doubtless in grief; one assumes as much. Why wouldn't this be the case? But their approach to the death is stoic. They understand that the work must go on. Winter is coming, and without enough logs for the woodstove, the family would freeze. They probably can't afford a hired hand, and the loss of this boy will be felt in his absence at work. But retreat isn't possible. The work must go on. This is, as noted above, a subsistence farm. The family "turned to their affairs," but this doesn't mean they have done so cheerfully. Quite the opposite. Their grief is folded into their work.

The poem takes its title from Shakespeare's *Macbeth*:

> Out, out, brief candle!
> Life's but a walking shadow, a poor player,
> That struts and frets his hour upon the stage,
> And then is heard no more. It is a tale
> Told by an idiot, full of sound and fury,
> Signifying nothing.

There is no saving imagery, no sentimentality, in Frost's poem. The poet lived and worked among rural people at the end of the nineteenth century, well into the twentieth, and he knew their ways, their approach to grieving, the sadness and the happiness that were part of their lives. This dramatic poem stays close to the narrative bone, a simple and swift unfolding of a story that puts forward a startling and upsetting scene, and it offers little in the way of consolation—apart from the poetry itself, which is thrilling to behold.

TWELVE

The Sound of Trees

I wonder about the trees.
Why do we wish to bear
Forever the noise of these
More than another noise
So close to our dwelling place?
We suffer them by the day
Till we lose all measure of pace,
And fixity in our joys,
And acquire a listening air.
They are that that talks of going
But never gets away;
And that talks no less for knowing,
As it grows wiser and older,
That now it means to stay.
My feet tug at the floor
And my head sways to my shoulder
Sometimes when I watch trees sway,
From the window or the door.
I shall set forth for somewhere,

I shall make the reckless choice
Some day when they are in voice
And tossing so as to scare
The white clouds over them on.
I shall have less to say,
But I shall be gone.

THIS CURIOUS but deeply memorable poem appears as the last poem in *Mountain Interval* (1916), and it shows the complexity of Frost's early work. "The Sound of Trees" is an extended metaphor, known as a conceit. The trees stand in for Frost's own restless nature, torn between liking "fixity" and wanting to move on, to "set forth for somewhere," anywhere. It's in some ways a poem that reflects the poet's own ambivalence toward home, even toward family, "our dwelling place." And there are autobiographical roots in this.

Having arrived back in the United States in 1915, the poet wondered what he should do. Was he famous enough to pursue a career in poetry? He wondered about giving readings. He was deeply shy, hesitant to speak in front of crowds. But that was a way to make a living in poetry, given the small sales that usually accompanied the publication of a slim volume. He settled quickly on another farm, in Franconia, high in the White Mountains of New Hampshire—this was, he thought, good for the allergies that seemed to plague his children. But it wasn't clear that he could make a living as a farmer, and he now had opportunities to teach. Amherst College invited him to come to its campus as a visiting poet for a term, and this proved a persuasive draw for him. He liked being home, and he also liked being away from home. And this tug of allegiances would continue to torment him for much of his adult life. He found it both satisfying and frustrating to stay at home, and the allure of getting away was always strong—he would read his poems on stages from coast to coast until the end of his life, even traveling to Europe, the Middle East, the Soviet Union, and South America. Nobody who looks at the life of Frost from any distance would say he stayed home too much.

"The Sound of Trees" is a skinny long poem, one that might even be said to look like a tree. The rhythm is steady and powerful, with a three-beat line. The rhyme scheme is odd and uneven, and—like "Storm Fear" and "After Apple-Picking," among other poems—the rhymes themselves seem like echoes; they somehow hold the poem in place without satisfying any typical pattern. The poem sways, and the rhymes are calculated to balance rootedness and chaos, a tension between rule and energy, which is perhaps also the major theme of this poem. The poet's farmhouse gives the speaker a fixed place in life, much as the roots of the trees fasten them to the soil. But there are consequences to being rooted that aren't all necessarily good.

Indeed, the sound of trees begins to trouble the speaker as he acquires this "listening air." They are "noise," after all—the word appears twice. And anyone who has lived under tall trees will understand the nature of this noise; as the wind blows through the branches and leaves, it sounds almost like whining voices. The narrator of the poem at first accepts the clamoring trees, and he's willing to withstand their insistence, their pestering sound. "We suffer them by the day" because we must. It's the wisdom of nature, after all. We grow attentive to their advice, which at first sounds like a good thing. They've been rooted in place for a good while, in a landscape that is home, so they might be thought of as elders.

The trees talk about "going," but the truth is, they're going nowhere. Trees don't travel. Yet they talk "no less for knowing" that they won't be going anywhere. In this, perhaps, they remind the speaker of those around him who pretend to great wisdom, who urge him to get into the world and do whatever he must to succeed, but who really don't themselves wish to leave. They most probably want the poet to stay put as well. It's in line fifteen that a kind of frustrated half acceptance of his fate occurs: "My feet tug at the floor / And my head sways to my shoulder." In effect, he becomes a tree himself. He's all "talk" of going, but he's really stuck. Nevertheless, there is a fierce determination in the poet, and it can't be suppressed: "I shall set forth for somewhere." He knows deep inside that he will "make the reckless choice" one day because he must.

The poem is a little story, a kind of natural fable, a metaphor in which the trees represent those around the speaker, his family and community. The trees are described as "that that talks of going," but if truth be told, they have never had any intention of getting away from the neighborhood where they're planted. They're rooted in one spot. This suggests a certain blustering hypocrisy in their tossing back and forth "to scare / The white clouds over them on." How can they be giving advice, anyway? The speaker grows distrustful of them. In a wry couplet at the end, the speaker establishes his independence: "I shall have less to say, / But I shall be gone."

One senses the growing frustration of the speaker, who must look through the windows and doors of his house without feeling good about the static and limited view. He wants out. Indeed, there is something contrary about him, as there was about Frost himself. He didn't wish to take advice. He deeply wanted to trust his own instincts, to keep his own counsel. Anyone could see this when he uprooted his family from the poultry farm in Derry in 1912 and moved the whole gang (including his wife and four young children) abroad, to England: a whimsical move, nothing that anyone could expect. Upon his return to New Hampshire, he found himself once again in a traveling mood.

THIRTEEN

Fire and Ice

Some say the world will end in fire,
Some say in ice.
From what I've tasted of desire
I hold with those who favor fire.
But if it had to perish twice,
I think I know enough of hate
To say that for destruction ice
Is also great
And would suffice.

THIS POEM from *New Hampshire* (1923) was written and first published in 1920. It's among the easiest and most satisfying of Frost's poems to commit to memory. In fact, reading it two or three times, it becomes impossible to forget. Frost's aphoristic talent is fiercely on display, and the poem feels like it should be framed, hung on the wall of the mind. It was one that Frost himself loved to read aloud, and he ended many readings with it.

A few years ago, in Vermont, I met a woman who encountered Frost in the early 1950s at the Bread Loaf Writers' Conference, not a mile or so from his farmhouse in Ripton, Vermont. Frost had been a kind of founding father of this conference, and he liked to give the final reading each summer in the Little Theater—a kind of tabernacle for poetry. As usual, he concluded with "Fire and Ice" on the night this woman was in attendance. Thunderous applause followed, and Frost rushed out through the west doors of the theater and walked to the bottom of the hill to have a moment by himself. He was smoking a cigarette, looking up at the stars, when this woman approached somewhat tentatively. She'd been told that he could be snippy.

"Excuse me, Mr. Frost, but may I ask a question?" she asked.

He looked at her warily. Who was this?

"It's about 'Fire and Ice,' the last poem you read," she added.

"What do you want to know?"

"I wonder what it means, Mr. Frost."

"What does it mean? I'll tell you." Then he thundered: "Some say the world will end in fire." He recited the whole poem again.

Frost made his point. The poem means what it says, and it's not a difficult poem to understand. With immense compression, Frost speculates about what people imagine the end of the world might look like. It's a poem about apocalyptic visions. And it has never seemed more relevant, in that we find ourselves in our time, more than a century after this poem was published, facing some terrifying options. There is fire, of course, which takes the form of burning landscapes, a result of climate change and other factors. It seems only too easy to imagine a world aflame. This combines with visions of a nuclear holocaust. We've all seen the images of Hiroshima and Nagasaki. In a brief instant, an atomic bomb could destroy everything we know and love.

It's also easy to imagine a frozen end to the world. We could well be moving into another ice age, which would destroy life as we know it. This is another possible consequence of climate change or nuclear war.

Nobody talked about climate change or nuclear weapons in 1920. These consequences of human action and invention lay decades in the future. But Frost knew that these two possibilities lay at hand, as much a product of the mind as anything else. The poet identifies fire with desire, its rhyme-word, and Frost was certainly not immune to furious passion. When his high school girlfriend and later wife, Elinor, seemed to reject him in 1894, he went briefly mad. He had already dropped out of Dartmouth and felt at a loss, his future uncertain. He wanted to marry Elinor, but she was a student at St. Lawrence University in upstate New York. Visiting her there unannounced, he got no fond reception. She wanted to finish college before she would think about marrying him. Convinced that she had another boyfriend, perhaps several, Frost took a merchant ship to Virginia and set off for an area known as the Great Dismal Swamp. He planned to end his life, perhaps, by drowning himself. The extent of his intentions remains unclear.

This was certainly a dark period in Frost's life, but it wasn't without positive aspects. Hez encountered several strangers along the way, and they offered help. Some hunters gave him food and shelter in a cabin. A hobo showed him how to hop freight trains. Making his way to Baltimore, Frost wired his mother, asking for money to get home, and she obliged. The world wasn't as bad a place as the young man had believed, and Elinor would soon enough marry him.

But by 1920 he again felt unclear about his future. Depression was a problem, and he didn't know what he could do to relieve its symptoms. Elinor was edgy, unhappy with her husband, who often left home to teach or give readings. Frost's only sibling, his sister, Jeanie, was committed to a mental asylum around this time, and the prognosis for her recovery wasn't good. Frost's mother—always a great support for him—had died. He had no sure footing in the world of literature or academe. He could all too easily fantasize about the end of the world.

If fire, for him, was desire, ice was associated with hate. Frost was never a cuddly figure, and he disliked many of the poets and professors he met. At Amherst, where he was teaching for one semester a year, he got into arguments with several professors on the faculty, whom he disliked intensely. (There was a particular colleague, a playwright named Stark Young, whom he especially despised.) In later years, he would go out of his way to make surly remarks about his fellow poets. In short, Frost could say without fear of exaggeration:

I think I know enough of hate
To say that for destruction ice
Is also great
And would suffice.

Frost was reading Dante at the time, and he understood about the bottom rung of hell, where ice and fire combined in lethal fashion. But there is, as ever, a whimsical side to Frost, and the tone here alleviates its dire content. Frost, to a degree, is making fun of those who prophesy in a doom-laden way. The world will come to an end, to be sure. Why wouldn't it? Does it really matter whether ice or fire carries us away?

A tightly rhymed, beautifully knotted poem of nine lines of variable length, "Fire and Ice" is both intensely personal and public, a kind of ironic pronouncement. Frost admits to his own desire, his own hate—both bad traits, as he knew—and he could see that these feelings might be multiplied in destructive ways. But just in saying this, he casts a rueful eye over all apocalyptic thinking, and he steps aside with a wink. The poem says what it means in a short space. And it resonates a century later, ever more relevant.

FOURTEEN

Stopping by Woods on a Snowy Evening

Whose woods these are I think I know.
His house is in the village though;
He will not see me stopping here
To watch his woods fill up with snow.

My little horse must think it queer
To stop without a farmhouse near
Between the woods and frozen lake
The darkest evening of the year.

He gives his harness bells a shake
To ask if there is some mistake.
The only other sound's the sweep
Of easy wind and downy flake.

The woods are lovely, dark and deep,
But I have promises to keep,
And miles to go before I sleep,
And miles to go before I sleep.

WRITTEN IN 1922, then included in *New Hampshire*, "Stopping by Woods on a Snowy Evening" might well be Frost's most iconic poem. It's a haunting and beautiful poem that should be part of the furniture of any well-educated mind. I committed its four quatrains to memory long ago—well over fifty years ago—and I've found myself repeating the poem for comfort, delight, and inspiration again and again. Its simple four-beat lines, which are iambic almost to a fault, fasten to an equally simple rhyme scheme, with the third line working as a connector to the next stanza, hence "here" links with "queer," "lake" joins hands with "shake," and "sweep" ties in with "deep." This interlocking technique is standard, in fact. Frost isn't breaking any new ground here.

This short poem with a long title is about a pause on a journey. The speaker sets off through the wintry woods at night in a horse-drawn sled. The fact of the sled and the horse dates the poem: we're in the world of the late nineteenth century or the very early twentieth, when this mode of transport would have been common in rural New England. Frost has scraped the poetic world of this poem clean of modern life. No cars. No flashing headlights. No airplane flying overhead among the stars. Just the dark woods, which "fill up with snow." This is, for the speaker, "The darkest evening of the year." This admission makes us wonder why everything is so dark. Surely there is a modicum of beauty in the frozen landscape. I have myself often paused in the woods near my rural farmhouse in Vermont to wonder at the falling snow, its softness, its purity. There is something glorious about snowy woods at night.

But Frost was going through a hard time. His sister was hospitalized for mental illness. He was himself battling depression, a problem that had also afflicted his mother before she died. Frost wrote a kind of companion poem to "Stopping by Woods" called "The Draft Horse," which didn't appear in print until 1962 when Frost included it in his final collection, *In the Clearing*, though in fact it was written much earlier—about the same time as "Stopping by Woods." In "The Draft Horse," a man not unlike the driver in "Stopping by Woods" moves "Through a pitch-dark limitless grove." The "night drew through the trees / In one long invidious draft." The speaker is also traveling in a horse-drawn sled. Suddenly an unknown figure leaps out of the darkness and "Deliberately stabbed him dead," meaning the horse. Why? It's a strange poem, utterly weird; I read it as a poem about depression, which could overwhelm Frost at any turn in the road. He was prone to bleak stretches, and in our day and age would probably have been given antidepressants. We can read this bleak midwinter mood back into "Stopping by Woods on a Snowy Evening."

The poem reflects on many things. I've always wondered about the man "in the village" who owns these woods. The speaker knows him, but clearly not very well. The driver of the sled is an invader here, a trespasser perhaps. These aren't his woods. Perhaps he is no longer even on the public road. In any case, why does he wish to stop in such an isolated place?

The horse "must think it queer." No farmhouse is near to offer consolation. The speaker seems to revel in his isolation, in the darkness itself that overwhelms him when he stops "Between the woods and frozen lake" on this dark night. The darkness is, indeed, a mental state here—a dark night of the soul.

Two of these lines have always been among my favorites: "The only other sound's the sweep / Of easy wind and downy flake." These lines are so effortless in the way they capture the essence of the moment. The sibilance of the diction captivates the ear, with "sound's the sweep." "Easy" remains an unlikely but perfect word to describe the wind, while "downy" is more familiar. Without the wind, there would be no "sweep," as snow usually falls in a silent way. The flakes are soft and downy, delicate. The whole scene is one of rapture.

But death as well seems present, or at least a kind of spiritual blankness. The woods, in their absolute loveliness, are "dark and deep." I'm reminded of some great lines from the Victorian poet Gerard Manley Hopkins here: "O the mind, mind has mountains; cliffs of fall / Frightful, sheer, no-man-fathomed." Hopkins, like Frost, suffered from dark periods, and his lines express the terror of the mind and its precipitous mountain ranges, with dangerous "cliffs of fall." "Dark and deep" modifies the "lovely" woods, forcing us to move away from accepting the beauty of the scene without its frightful depths and darkness. I suspect we have all known these woods, at once "lovely, dark and deep." And, like Frost or his speaker, we have willed ourselves forward.

Frost's poem offers great encouragement. "But I have promises to keep" suggests that, however bitter and cold the night may seem, however much one might wish to disappear into the forest, fade from being, there are responsibilities and "promises to keep." I find this heartening, even thrilling. The poet insists on the need to hold fast to our word, to believe in further commitments. There are covenants we accept, as human beings, and they must be fulfilled.

The simple repetition works to implant the lines in the collective memory: "And miles to go before I sleep, / And miles to go before I sleep." Frost imposes on the reader the necessity of lowering volume and pitch to make the repeated line creditable as speech: the voicing becomes more private, internal, contemplative—as though the speaker were taking on board all the possible resonances. John F. Kennedy, when he was campaigning for the presidency in 1960, often ended a speech with these lines. It was a way of ending a political speech, of course, and getting out of the room. But it was also a way of saying that he had promises to keep, promises to the nation, and that he wouldn't stop until he had fulfilled them. The "sleep" here might, simply, refer to a restful night. It might also relate to death. The poet/speaker wills himself forward, knowing he has things to accomplish before his final "sleep."

Few poems are more perfect or magically resonant than "Stopping by Woods on a Snowy Evening," which Frost himself once described as his "best bid" for immortality. The poem doesn't answer questions—it raises them. Who really owns the woods? I doubt Frost thought much about the man in town who had the legal deed to them. After all, isn't it the man who beholds the woods in deep appreciation who has the real deed? Why did the driver stop to watch the woods "fill up with snow"? Was he depressed, or was this an antidote to depression, a willingness to absorb the darkness, the snow, the "easy wind," which is the spirit blowing over the world? (Frost would know that "wind" in Latin is *spiritus*.) What promises does he wish to keep? What is the nature of the sleep that must follow a long journey? How does one take up the "miles to go" without despair? It's enough to have these questions, to hear them posed in a way that, like all great art, creates a unified and definite impression.

FIFTEEN

Design

I found a dimpled spider, fat and white,
On a white heal-all, holding up a moth
Like a white piece of rigid satin cloth—
Assorted characters of death and blight
Mixed ready to begin the morning right,
Like the ingredients of a witches' broth—
A snow-drop spider, a flower like a froth,
And dead wings carried like a paper kite.

What had that flower to do with being white,
The wayside blue and innocent heal-all?
What brought the kindred spider to that height,
Then steered the white moth thither in the night?
What but design of darkness to appall?—
If design govern in a thing so small.

FIRST PUBLISHED in *American Poetry, 1922: A Miscellany* and later included in Frost's collection *A Further Range* (1936), "Design" is a sonnet that challenges the idea of God as a benevolent creator-spirit. It's a poem of tremendous intellectual and emotional depth, one that forces us to think hard about the nature of the universe, whether it was "designed" or not. It goes further: Might a designer have been malevolent? How else can one explain the horrible things one sees? As usual, Frost doesn't give us easy answers. In this poem, he presents a picture of reality—not a pretty picture—and leaves it to readers to contemplate and assess.

The great theologian Thomas Aquinas famously put forward the "argument from design" in the thirteenth century. He argues that, given the intricate complexity of the world, it must have been put together by a Designer, who is God. Aquinas says we must look closely at the world, observing how things are put together. Order is everything to him, and he finds both order and deftness. This argument is also called the "teleological argument," meaning that an appreciation for design in creation leads to a sense of the end (*telos* in Greek) or purpose of the universe. Frost was hardly the first to challenge this argument—one might look up David Hume's rebuttal of Aquinas, for instance—but Frost's poem is nonetheless bold, even shocking, in its implications.

This poem is a sonnet built on the Italian (or Petrarchan) model, with an octave and a sestet. In the octave, as usual, the poet creates in eight lines an image. In the sestet, which contains six lines, he interrogates or reflects on this image. The rhymed couplet at the end, which offers a real zinger in this case, draws a bit on the Shakespearean sonnet, which tended to conclude with a moral or reflection, a summary judgment. But the "feel" of this sonnet, especially its architecture, is Italian.

The poem begins with a simple image from nature: "I found a dimpled spider, fat and white, / On a white heal-all, holding up a moth." This is a white-on-white image: the white spider, the white flower, and the white moth. White is a symbol of purity, of course; but it's also associated with death, as in a funeral pall—the cloth (usually white) that covers a casket. In this case, Frost gives us a "dimpled spider, fat and white." This is, to be frank, a disgusting image. A baby should be dimpled and fat, not a spider. There's a cringe factor from the outset. Now we add the "white heal-all." This is normally a blue flower, the prunella, seen commonly by the roadside in New England. Rarely would this flower be white, so Frost gives us an aberration of some kind. The world is out of joint. Then comes the moth, now compared to "a white piece of rigid satin cloth," which again recalls a funeral pall. Not a pleasant image.

This combination of spider with flower and moth is compared to the ingredients of "a witches' broth," which has been "Mixed ready to begin the morning right." The latter phrase seems more appropriate for a breakfast cereal, and Frost seems to delight in the jaunty expression. It's possibly a line taken from a radio ad for a cereal, in fact. Yet this is hardly a way to begin the morning with a smile. In a summary of sorts, Frost summons the image in its parts: "A snow-drop spider, a flower like a froth, / And dead wings carried like a paper kite." That "flower like a froth" has always unnerved me: the froth seems like a sickly froth spewing from the mouth of someone who has fainted. There is nothing cozy about this flower, nothing pretty. And the dead wings are "carried" like a kite, a symbol of death and blight—and the childhood kite does nothing to alleviate the horror.

The image is complete, and now Frost interrogates it, making a sharp turn (volta) into the sestet:

> What had that flower to do with being white,
> The wayside blue and innocent heal-all?
> What brought the kindred spider to that height,
> Then steered the white moth thither in the night?

That flower should not be white. So much for the innocent bloom—part of the mint family—that one sees in New England. And then "the kindred spider" is summoned, with a kind of eerie familial association. Death aligns with death. Who put together this image, such a combination of unpleasant factors, and "steered the white moth thither" in the sky? The archaic word "thither" has a biblical aura. But there are no supernatural forces at work here ... are there? Maybe there are. But if so, can we imagine these forces could be benign? That seems unlikely.

The last couplet summarizes the poem: "What but design of darkness to appall?— / If design govern in a thing so small."

That is, if nature in its little parts has been assembled in a way that drains the blood from the cheeks—as in the word "appall"—then perhaps some malevolent Creator has designed this bleak instance. Being a student of Latin, Frost knew of course that "appall" comes from a Latin word meaning "to make white or pale." Certainly the appalling image before us creates fear, anxiety, and distress. In a brilliant essay on Frost in *Poetry and the Age* (1953), the poet-critic Randall Jarrell suggests that the ending of "Design," with its fierce summing-up, "comes as something taken for granted, a relief almost, in its mere statement and generalization, after the almost unbearable actuality and particular of what has come before." Or possibly it's just a punch in the gut?

This is surely one of the most terrifying poems in English. Sometimes we memorize a poem not to comfort or cheer us, as with many of Frost's poems, but to steel us as we face a dark universe. I've often said this line to myself in times of stress: "What but design of darkness to appall?" It's not to make myself feel better that I repeat the line. I say it to brace myself for what comes next, what is inevitable, a bald truth that is couched in some of the finest language in American literature.

SIXTEEN

Directive

Back out of all this now too much for us,
Back in a time made simple by the loss
Of detail, burned, dissolved, and broken off
Like graveyard marble sculpture in the weather,
There is a house that is no more a house
Upon a farm that is no more a farm
And in a town that is no more a town.
The road there, if you'll let a guide direct you
Who only has at heart your getting lost,
May seem as if it should have been a quarry—
Great monolithic knees the former town
Long since gave up pretense of keeping covered.
And there's a story in a book about it:
Besides the wear of iron wagon wheels
The ledges show lines ruled southeast northwest,
The chisel work of an enormous Glacier
That braced his feet against the Arctic Pole.
You must not mind a certain coolness from him
Still said to haunt this side of Panther Mountain.

Nor need you mind the serial ordeal
Of being watched from forty cellar holes
As if by eye pairs out of forty firkins.
As for the woods' excitement over you
That sends light rustle rushes to their leaves,
Charge that to upstart inexperience.
Where were they all not twenty years ago?
They think too much of having shaded out
A few old pecker-fretted apple trees.
Make yourself up a cheering song of how
Someone's road home from work this once was,
Who may be just ahead of you on foot
Or creaking with a buggy load of grain.
The height of the adventure is the height
Of country where two village cultures faded
Into each other. Both of them are lost.
And if you're lost enough to find yourself
By now, pull in your ladder road behind you
And put a sign up CLOSED to all but me.
Then make yourself at home. The only field
Now left's no bigger than a harness gall.
First there's the children's house of make believe,
Some shattered dishes underneath a pine,
The playthings in the playhouse of the children.
Weep for what little things could make them glad.
Then for the house that is no more a house,
But only a belilaced cellar hole,
Now slowly closing like a dent in dough.

This was no playhouse but a house in earnest.
Your destination and your destiny's
A brook that was the water of the house,
Cold as a spring as yet so near its source,
Too lofty and original to rage.
(We know the valley streams that when aroused
Will leave their tatters hung on barb and thorn.)
I have kept hidden in the instep arch
Of an old cedar at the waterside
A broken drinking goblet like the Grail
Under a spell so the wrong ones can't find it,
So can't get saved, as Saint Mark says they mustn't.
(I stole the goblet from the children's playhouse.)
Here are your waters and your watering place.
Drink and be whole again beyond confusion.

WRITTEN WHEN the poet was in his seventies, "Directive" appears in *Steeple Bush* (1947), and it's a massive achievement, a culminating work in which Frost revisits his life, offering a late take on art, mortality, and the life of the spirit. It falls into the category of the Greater Romantic Lyric—a term coined by M. H. Abrams in 1965, elaborated in a later book called *The Correspondent Breeze* (1984). Coleridge, Keats, Tennyson, and many other poets from the nineteenth century wrote poems that fall into this category (as did several modern poets, including Stevens and Auden), but the most iconic is Wordsworth's "Tintern Abbey."

Such a poem is a meditative one, set in nature, often about a return to a place where inspiration was once found and will be discovered again. Such poems have a broad spiritual aspiration, tilting toward what Wordsworth called "a sense sublime / Of something far more deeply interfused, / Whose dwelling is the light of setting suns." "Directive" is Frost's gesture in this direction, a hugely ambitious work unlike anything else in Frost.

It's a difficult poem, in its way, offering a blizzard of hidden allusions, moving in various directions as the poet-speaker seeks guidance. It begins with two astonishing rolling parallel clauses marked by slyly contrasting prepositions ("Back out . . . Back in. . ."). The reference in the first line to Wordsworth is clear: "The world is too much with us," the earlier poet wrote in a sonnet by the same name. The Industrial Revolution had ruined the world of nature, for Wordsworth. Frost feels the same dismay, yearning for "a time made simple by the loss / Of detail." The exact details have been, in the mind, "broken off / Like graveyard marble sculpture in the weather."

A graveyard is not an uncommon site for poetry by poets. But time weathers the granite monuments. The elaborations— probably even the names and dates—are worn away. Memory itself does the work of simplification. And here Frost summons a farmhouse in the country, perhaps like one that he and his family first inhabited in Derry, New Hampshire. Now it's "a house that is no more a house" and it will be found on "a farm that is no more a farm." It's "in a town that is no more a town" because all this lies in the past, which is no country one can visit in a literal sense. You can't go home again. But this poem offers a "directive," a map of sorts, a field guide to experience, and there is a mysterious guide (the poet and not him) who wants "you," perhaps the speaker but also the reader, to return with him in time. He's not the usual guide, since he "only has at heart your getting lost," a phrase that gestures toward the Christian paradox of getting lost in order to be found.

Nature, the vast ecosphere of this poem, is personified. We encounter "Great monolithic knees" that poke up like blades of granite through the soil. The guide revisits the geological origins of the landscape, with a massive glacier pushing its feet against the North Pole and stretching out, scraping the surface of the words, leaving dents and bruises as the landscape is "chiseled" into being. This great icy beast may still "haunt this side of Panther Mountain." Frost summons a complicated world of ancient "iron wagon wheels." There's "a story in a book" about all of this, although we don't know what book this might be.

There's an ordeal by memory here, more ice than fire, as we suffer an atmosphere of "coolness" "this side of Panther Mountain," and we undergo the frightening "serial ordeal / Of being watched from forty cellar holes / As if by eye pairs out of forty firkins." These are houses that have sunken almost out of sight, a village fallen into "cellar holes" that feel like empty barrels or "firkins." Going back into the world of memory is hard. It's easier to forget the past, pretend it never happened. But the spiritual quest that Frost initiates isn't one of ease, no "easy gold at the hand of fay or elf," as he wrote in "Mowing." It's about confronting the past—its good and bad sides—and taking inspiration there.

We're in the woods in the poem, at last. And there is conso-
lation there, although one has to be careful. "As for the woods'
excitement over you / That sends light rustle rushes to their
leaves, / Charge that to upstart inexperience." One has to be
versed in country things to realize that nature isn't talking to
us, isn't trying to teach us something, doesn't just want to cheer
us on. It's important, Frost seems to suggest, to remain realistic,
alert, open to whatever happens as one proceeds on this quest.

Frost leaps sideways now, reviving a world of twenty years or
even longer before, coming upon a stand of "old pecker-fretted
apple trees." As a fruit farmer himself, in Vermont mostly, Frost
knew these trees, with the marks made by woodpeckers. The
walker in these mystical woods now can perhaps make up "a
cheering song" of how this road was once somebody's "road
home from work." Indeed, that person may be just up ahead,
on foot, or driving a horse-cart "with a buggy load of grain."
This was indeed "The height of the adventure" in the old days, a
well-traveled country road.

Frost (or the speaker in his poem) has climbed a hill, and he
arrives at a place where two villages once blended, faded, disap-
peared into each other, then vanished altogether. It's a sobering
story, a dream of erasure. It's not necessarily a nightmare, as
there is nostalgia here. Frost would have once stood in such
places, and he might even have sensed the fading of these cul-
tures as he stood there. Nothing stays put. But now he's on his
own, with his guide, and the reader is over his shoulder.

Frost writes: "And if you're lost enough to find yourself / By
now, pull in your ladder road behind you / And put a sign up

CLOSED to all but me." That is, once you're deeply lost in a way that, paradoxically, allows you to be found, then you can submit fully to the guide, even to the quest-poem itself. Then you can "make yourself at home" in this diminished place where what was once a big hay field has become "no bigger than a harness gall." Nature has closed in, surrounded the speaker. As Frost wanders into the woods, he finds something amazing: the final scene of the poem, a house that stands in for "home."

It's a house where he once—or might have—lived with his wife and four surviving children. First there's a "house of make believe," a kind of "playhouse," with "Some shattered dishes underneath a pine." There are toys scattered about, "playthings in the playhouse of the children." One can feel the pressure of the poet's emotion here as he reviews these objects. So much is gone. His wife, Elinor, is dead: she died in 1938. Frost's beloved daughter Marjorie died in childbirth, four years before Frost lost his wife. His son Carol shot himself in 1940, a terrible suicide, totally unexpected. Irma, another daughter, was clearly unstable, and she would be committed to a mental asylum in 1947, the year "Directive" was published. Frost is, in his seventies, on his own. And the farmhouse he once loved "is no more a house"; it's nothing but a hole in the ground with lilacs, the flowers of nostalgia, circling it: "a belilaced cellar hole."

But this was, once upon a time, "a house in earnest." The family made a life there, and it was a good life, in its way. And near that house was a brook, not unlike the brook in "Hyla Brook," a source of inspiration, a personal Helicon. It's wonderfully described as "Cold as a spring as yet so near its source,

/ Too lofty and original to rage." I've always thought that Frost referred to his own poetry here. It was not a poetry of "rage." It was, indeed, "lofty and original." Of course Frost knows the danger: these streams can flood, and "leave their tatters hung on barb and thorn." But the waters of the stream are essential. They are the source.

Frost always felt a rivalry with T. S. Eliot, and he never liked the pompous allusions of *The Waste Land*. This was not his style. Now he gestures in Eliot's direction. The Fisher King in *The Waste Land* was seen to be searching for the Holy Grail—the original cup that Jesus used for communion on the night before he was crucified. In the Middle Ages, there was a famous search for this Grail. If you found it, the dry lands around you would be restored. The quest for this Grail is a quest for redemption, a way of setting your lands in order, as Eliot suggests. So it's with some irony that the Grail in Frost becomes "A broken drinking goblet" that is just sitting by the stream. Frost's speaker says he has kept this goblet "hidden in the instep arch / Of an old cedar at the waterside." It's "Under a spell," he says, and this is "so the wrong ones can't find it."

The "wrong ones" are those in the fourth chapter of the Gospel of Mark, where Jesus talks about those who understand the world only as parables and can't see through them to the truth of the stories. They can't listen to Jesus, can't hear the truth in his tales. There is a secret mystery. One must (so Jesus seems to suggest) give up one's normal life, move beyond simple and nostalgic tales of the past, digging more deeply than ever before into the mysteries. The truth is available to those who deign to listen, who take up the cross and follow Jesus, submitting to the wisdom of the scriptures. But it's not easy. And nor is "Directive" an easy poem. It's full of wisdom, of course; but one must give up something as one gives in to the poem, making it part of oneself. Frost invites us to walk beside him, to become our guide. And his readers, who have followed him on this circuitous quest into the dark woods of memory, must accept the possibilities of learning something essential.

The poem ends with two of the most quotable lines in all of Frost: "Here are your waters and your watering place. / Drink and be whole again beyond confusion." In "The Figure a Poem Makes," Frost describes poetry as "a momentary stay against confusion." And for him, confusion was the order of the day. Life was generally "a pathless wood," as he says in "Birches." The world was too much with him. It was all too much. But there is a source, in memory, where one can recover meaning and find inspiration in the deepest sense. Frost has been here before, hiding the goblet in the tree's "instep arch." He knows where to go. We go back there with him and drink from these waters. And we become, in the final moment, "whole again beyond confusion." The poem moves toward a clarification of life. We're suddenly in a clearing, a mental and spiritual clearing, and it's because we have followed this poem to the end.

Tips on Memorization

1. Make memorization a part of your daily routine. Taking just ten or fifteen minutes out of your day to follow these steps will enable you to memorize many poems. Don't be discouraged if you miss a day here or there but try to get into a routine.

2. First read through the poem slowly for comprehension. Reread it, and then read it aloud a couple of times.

3. Using a playing card or a folded piece of paper, cover all the lines in the poem except for the first line, read it aloud, and then look away from the page and say the line to yourself a few times. Repeat this process, proceeding one line at a time; however, you should never feel you have to memorize the *whole* poem in a single sitting. Think in terms of stanzas or discreet chunks—sentences or smaller syntactic units.

4. Once you have memorized one stanza or chunk, move on to the next until you come to the end of the poem.

5. Copy the poem onto a sheet of paper or type it into a Word document. Compare what you've written to the original. The goal is to lodge the poem in your memory.

6. Take advantage of "stolen time" to recite the poem: in the shower or in the car, while walking the dog or taking other

exercise—wherever you happen to find yourself alone with sufficient head space.

7. When trying to memorize longer poems, try the "mind palace" technique: visualize each line of the poem—or rather a keyword in it—as an object in a room, so that as you recall these objects from left to right, each line will return to you. Place each stanza or syntactic unit in a different room in your mind palace. Your palace should be modeled on your home or another space familiar to you, so that the sequence in which you visit these rooms reflects your natural movements.

8. Remember there's no shame in committing to memory only those parts of a poem that convey its wisdom or that speak to you personally.

RECOMMENDATIONS
FOR FURTHER READING

Frost, Robert. *The Letters of Robert Frost, Volume 1: 1886–1920*, edited by Donald Sheehy, Mark Richardson, and Robert Faggen. Cambridge, MA: Belknap Press, 2014.

Frost, Robert. *The Letters of Robert Frost, Volume 2: 1920–1928*, edited by Donald Sheehy, Mark Richardson, Robert Bernard Hass, and Henry Atmore. Cambridge, MA: Belknap Press, 2016.

Frost, Robert. *The Letters of Robert Frost, Volume 3: 1929–1936*, edited by Mark Richardson, Donald Sheehy, Robert Bernard Hass, and Henry Atmore. Cambridge, MA: Belknap Press, 2021.

Frost, Robert. *The Notebooks of Robert Frost*, edited by Robert Faggen. Cambridge, MA: Belknap Press, 2007.

Frost, Robert. *Robert Frost: Collected Poems, Prose, & Plays*. New York: Library of America, 1995.

Orr, David. *The Road Not Taken: Finding America in the Poem Everyone Loves and Almost Everyone Gets Wrong*. New York: Penguin Press, 2015.

Parini, Jay. *Robert Frost: A Life*. New York: Henry Holt & Company, 1999.

ABOUT THE AUTHOR

© Oliver Parini

JAY PARINI is a poet, novelist, biographer, screenwriter, and critic. He is the author of six books of poetry, including *The Art of Subtraction* and *New and Collected Poems, 1975–2015,* and eight novels, including *Benjamin's Crossing, The Damascus Road, The Apprentice Lover, The Passages of H.M.,* and *The Last Station*—the latter was made into an Academy Award–nominated film and translated into over thirty languages. He has written biographies of Robert Frost, John Steinbeck, William Faulkner, Gore Vidal, and Jesus. His other works include *The Art of Teaching, Why Poetry Matters, Promised Land: Thirteen Books that Changed America, The Way of Jesus,* and *Borges and Me: An Encounter.* Among his many edited volumes are the *Oxford Encyclopedia of American Literature, The Norton Book of American Autobiography, The Columbia Anthology of American Poetry,* and *The Columbia History of American Poetry.* He lives in Weybridge, Vermont, and has been on the faculty of Middlebury College since 1982. He is married to Devon Jersild, a clinical psychologist and writer, and they have three sons.

This book is set in 11-point Adobe Jenson, a serif typeface created by award-winning designer Robert Slimbach and released in 1996. Distinguished by its low "x" height, the lettering is based on a typeface cut in Venice in the 1470s by Nicolas Jenson, a book printer still celebrated for perfecting the form of roman type. The italics are inspired by a style designed in Rome a half century later by Ludovico Vicentino degli Arrighi, a papal scribe whose legacy is a series of italic typefaces modeled after chancery script.

Text design and composition by Gopa & Ted2, Inc. Albuquerque, NM. Cover and endpaper design by Kimberly Glyder. Printing and binding by Lakeside Book Company.